Liberalism

KEY CONCEPTS

Published

Liberalism

Paul Kelly

polity

First published in 2005 by Polity Press

Polity Press
65 Bridge Street
Cambridge CB2 1UR, UK.

Polity Press
350 Main Street
Malden, MA 02148, USA

ISBN: 0-7456-3290-4
ISBN: 0-7456-3291-2 (paperback)

A catalogue record for this book is available from the British Library

Typeset in 10^1/$_2$ on 12 pt Sabon
by SNP Best-set Typesetter Ltd., Hong Kong
Printed and bound in Great Britain by MPG Books Ltd, Bodmin, Cornwall

For further information on Polity, visit our website: www.polity.co.uk

Contents

For G. W. and P. J. Kelly,
my parents

Preface and Acknowledgements

There are many books on liberalism; all have something in common, yet all are different in important respects. If all political theories and ideologies had a single uncontroversial character there would be far fewer books and much less for political theorists to do. Fortunately, political theories do not have such a stable character. There is always room for revisionism and redescription. That is part of the rationale for this book. I offer an account of liberalism as a normative political theory. In doing this I take a position on what is essential and relevant, and what is not important, or of merely historical interest. Consequently, some readers will be surprised that I do not address some of their preferred liberal gurus. But my aim is not to offer a comprehensive survey of all possible liberal sources and thinkers. I do not think such a project is possible. That said, my approach is not merely arbitrary and self-serving. The type of liberalism I address is alive and commonplace in contemporary political philosophy and theory. Like it, or loathe it, it cannot be ignored. Yet, equally, it should not be mistaken for other variants of liberalism with which it significantly differs. Its widespread currency, and persistent confusion or conflation with other theories and movements, suggested that there was indeed scope for yet another book on liberalism. For a number of years, my own students at LSE have sought such a short, book-length account of political liberalism, so they are in part to blame for what follows. They are not wholly to blame. The book also emerged out of lectures and seminars given at the CEU in Budapest, Peking University in Beijing, and universities in Fukuoka and Tokyo. The experience in all these venues encouraged me to think that the ideas of citizen equality that are at the heart of political liberalism are not solely the fantasies of privileged ivory-tower academics from the Atlantic democracies. I am grateful to my hosts on these occasions: Professor Andras Sajo, Professor Qiang Li and Professor Seki. I am particularly grateful for their generosity – something increasingly difficult to reciprocate in British universities.

A number of people deserve special mention. Brian Barry took time to read this when under pressure to finish a book of his own. As ever, I am grateful to his generosity and sage advice (and that of Anni Parker). Matt Clayton read and commented on the manuscript for Polity. His report was a model of good sense. I have endeavoured to accommodate all of his criticisms, and where I have not followed his advice, it should not indicate disagreement. The book could have been longer, more thorough and better written. At Polity I have benefited from the enthusiasm of Louise Knight and the assistance of Andrea Drugan. David Held, as both publisher and colleague, also deserves special mention. He is a wonderfully supportive and enthusiastic colleague, who has helped make Polity a first-choice publisher for political theorists. It is also convenient to have a publisher down the corridor. That said, he could have declined the book. He didn't and I am very grateful.

Finally, and perhaps curiously for a book on liberal egalitarianism, family played an important part in this book. Over many years now, I have been engaged in a continuing argument with my parents, often about issues addressed in this book. They were my first teachers in moral and political thinking and I continue to learn from them. They instilled a passionate interest in what turned out to be political theory and they have remained interested in, if not always convinced by, what I have learnt along the way. This book is for them. I have also learnt from my own children, Tom and Ruth, as they become adults. They have discussed and argued over many of the issues in this book. Although they may not be able to see where I have tried to answer their questions, I can. My wife Anne continues to be a sceptical interlocutor and the mainstay and support of all that I do. This is perhaps a pretty poor return for her good humour, support and patience. Yet family is not everything; in writing this book I enjoyed the companionship of two cats. They contributed to this book in ways that only cats can.

1
Introduction: What is Liberalism?

Liberalism is a precarious achievement of enduring value. This important legacy of both European history and philosophy – what we sometimes like to abbreviate imprecisely as the Enlightenment – is not simply of local significance to the Atlantic democracies and their close relatives such as Australia and New Zealand. It has a scope and resonance that continues to inspire political emancipation both within Europe and far beyond. Furthermore, it is an achievement that is not subject to the increasingly commonplace charges of philosophical confusion, reductionist individualism, political naivete and irrelevance, or cultural imperialism, or, at least, that is what I contend in what follows. This book offers a restatement and defence of liberalism as a theory about the proper limits to the exercise of political power and about the scope of just political action. Yet liberalism is ubiquitous in both the academy and the public realm, so much so that it is often presented as a hegemonic ideology or intellectual orthodoxy, so why do we need another defence of liberalism? In answering this simple question we open up issues that take us to the heart of the problem of liberalism as an ideology, political movement or approach to normative political theory. The short answer to this question is that most current books on the subject tend to bury liberalism rather than praise it (or at least defend it).[1]

Historians of political thought or ideology often weave complex and interesting tales, attempting to combine ideology, political movements and philosophical position into a coherent whole. Such narratives are always deeply unsatisfactory to someone. Just as Marxists always tend to dismiss characterizations of Marxism as incomplete, partial or distorting, so liberals are equally prone to dispute any attempt to get to the core of what liberalism is really about. So any book that sets out to defend liberalism is bound to face the charge that it offers a distortion, caricature or incomplete picture, that when looked at from another angle shows precisely the opposite of what is depicted. As with many contemporary political concepts and ideologies, liberalism is a deeply contested notion, not least among liberals themselves. A proper history of liberalism would have to try and disentangle the central components of this contested tradition or ideological form. Fortunately I am not concerned with offering *the* history of liberalism as a single ideological form. For a variety of reasons, which are not central to my argument in this book, I do not think such a single history is possible. There is a variety of different national stories that one could tell about liberalism in different countries. Each of these histories emphasizes different concepts, key thinkers and political developments. All of these different national stories are interesting and enhance our understanding of the resources and influences of a complex set of political traditions and arguments. I draw on some of this material selectively in what follows. However, I do not wish to claim that there is a single, true core vision of liberalism. Nor am I concerned with providing a historical account of liberalism as such, although history will play some part in the account of liberalism I present.

Establishing the identity of any historical tradition or ideology is no simple task, if it is even a coherent enterprise. Many contemporary historians of political ideas warn us that ideologies are not really the kinds of things that serious historians should be concerned with.[2] Mindful of this warning and also aware of the need to avoid similar philosophical pitfalls, I claim no more than that the subject of this book is one among a variety of approaches that one can call liberalism.[3] I am concerned with liberalism as a normative political theory, or what with more precision might be called political liberalism. Political liberalism is a branch of the broader liberal tradition that places liberal-egalitarianism distributive principles at its core. It is political for the reason that it is intended to accommodate the plurality of different views about how individuals should live their lives. It does not offer a full theory of personal morality, but instead places limits on the variety of moral and political perspectives that are found in modern democratic societies. These limits are determined by its core normative commitment to the equal status and treatment of each person. Forms of life or third-person moral claims (how I think others should live) are acceptable as public reasons only as long as they are compatible with the recognition of the equal status of others. I can argue for and campaign for my views about how others should live, but I cannot use the power of the state to bring them around to my views. Political liberalism involves the recognition of equal status and what is often referred to as the strategy of privatization. That is the recognition of the need to make controversial moral, political and religious views a matter of private concern, rather than a source of public political conflict. It is important to note, at this point, that political liberalism does not entail moral scepticism. Political liberalism is a moralized political theory; it derives from a recognition of the equal moral worth and standing of all individuals, but it also claims that this view places limits on the scope of moral claims given the fact of reasonable pluralism of moral views in modern democratic societies.

I do not claim that this is all there is to liberalism, nor do I claim that the history of liberalism as a political movement inevitably culminates in contemporary liberal egalitarianism. I wish that were so but it is not. What I am offering here is not a history of the inevitable unfolding of the true character of liberalism. For some, what I defend here will be seen as only a partial offshoot of the liberal family, or even a perversion of classical liberalism. It is merely the current fashion of contemporary political theory since the publication of John Rawls' *A Theory of Justice* in 1971. One might argue that an alternative 'epistemological' variant of liberalism, associated with the names of Hayek and Popper, is much closer to the older tradition of classical liberalism, stretching back to the nineteenth century. This epistemological liberalism is still very much alive, although it has indeed been partially eclipsed by Rawlsian political liberalism. However one characterizes liberalism, certain major figures will command attention. I could have told a story that places J. S. Mill, Friedrich Hayek, or Karl Popper at centre stage. Instead, as will soon become clear, my story places John Rawls at centre stage. Alongside Rawls, I also draw on the ideas of Ronald Dworkin and Brian Barry, both of whom develop and extend the Rawlsian legacy. This might be seen to give a peculiarly North American flavour to my account of liberalism. Indeed, some commentators, such as John Gray, have argued that Rawls' legacy has had the negative effect of crowding out other important voices from European liberalism.[4] While there is something to Gray's charge, it remains a distortion to see Rawls' legacy as narrowly north American. Instead the model of liberal egalitarianism he develops is deeply rooted in the European tradition and, perhaps most interestingly, British moral and political theory.

Given all these reasons, it is important to acknowledge that any single interpretation of a complex historical tradition of thought and practice will remain deeply contested. For this reason I want to lower my claims for the variant of liberalism I shall discuss in the rest of this book. Yet I do not want to say that it is merely a contingency of personal taste or prejudice that has made me focus on the political liberalism of Rawls and his followers, rather than the epistemological liberalism of Hayek or Popper. My reasons for focusing on political liberalism are not its historical inevitability, but rather its current political and philosophical significance, which for good or ill cannot be seriously doubted. Whatever its ultimate provenance, liberal egalitarianism remains, in my view, that within the liberal tradition that is most attractive, compelling and least subject to the charge of redundancy. Its appropriateness to the modern democratic state is part of the reason for its hold on the imagination of political theorists in the anglophone world. Whether this connection with the modern democratic state makes the liberal perspective 'the only game in town', the end of history, or merely a contingency that is in the process of giving way to less state-centred forms of political association, is a highly contested topic and one I shall be concerned with in the final section of this book.[5] That said, in a world in which fear of external threats, real or imagined, has put all other political issues on hold, it is more important than ever to recover and restate the principles that derive from liberal egalitarianism and to free ourselves from the corrosive effects of the spurious elevation of community, culture, and majority public opinion over the claims for the equal moral standing of all individuals, whoever they are and wherever they come from.

The conception of liberalism I describe and defend in this book is unfortunately not widely credited in the real world of contemporary democratic politics. Indeed, it has become increasingly fashionable to disparage it. All too frequently, the popular US practice of using the term 'liberal' as a form of political abuse is adopted by both the press and so-called left-of-centre politicians, even in Britain. It is also a common practice, amongst those who should know better, to dismiss concerns about the curtailment of civil liberties as merely the hand-wringing of 'bleeding heart' liberals. What is most disturbing about these responses is that they are not merely the knee-jerk reactions of right-wing commentators and conservative politicians, but are increasingly commonplace amongst those on the left. Yet the liberal egalitarianism they criticize or dismiss is the only adequate principled response that those on the left have to the tyranny of majority opinion and the coercive imposition of arbitrary power. If it does not remain central to the political movement of social democracy, then that tradition has nothing to recommend it beyond its somewhat equivocal history and failure in the economic realm to offer a viable alternative to the marketplace, neither of which are particularly strong selling points.

Another perhaps more surprising realm in which liberal egalitarianism is in retreat is that of the academy. Why this is surprising is that post-Rawlsian liberal egalitarianism is supposed to be the ruling orthodoxy or paradigm for political theory in the anglophone world. Liberalism is often used as a euphemism or shorthand for political theory, ever since the publication of Rawls' *A Theory of Justice* finally contradicted Peter Laslett's premature obituary for political philosophy.[6] Many political theorists still write laments about the difficulty of moving out from beneath Rawls' long shadow, and will no doubt be surprised by my claim that liberal egalitarianism is in retreat in the academy. Yet the hegemonic role of Rawlsian political liberalism is more an appearance than a reality. Non-Rawlsian perspectives still predominate in the teaching and study of political theory, and where the Rawlsian legacy of liberal egalitarianism is defended this is usually in dry-as-dust 'micro-debates' about minor arguments concerning particular pages of *A Theory of Justice*. Liberal egalitarianism is worthy but dull, and no match for the more exciting and esoteric reaches of post-structuralism and deconstructionism, or the flirtation with danger offered by the likes of Nietzsche or Carl Schmitt. Even amongst the worthy, the lure of libertarianism, communitarianism or multiculturalism continues to challenge the coherence and desirability of political liberalism.

As a *liberal* egalitarian I cannot, and do not want to, deny that this plurality of voices is both beneficial and important. It is no part of liberal egalitarianism's aspiration to offer itself as a dogmatic truth beyond the necessary challenges of rival views. That said, the tendency of liberal egalitarianism to become increasingly concerned with the *minutiae* of Rawls or Dworkin, places a responsibility on other sympathetic critics to try to renew interest in the broader liberal egalitarian position. That is primarily what I aim to offer in this short book – not a full philosophical or sociological defence of the liberal egalitarian perspective. Instead my aim is to provide an overview and endorsement of the liberal egalitarian perspective, and dismissal of some of the standard arguments for its supposed philosophical incoherence or political redundancy.

This task is both important and urgent if it is to retain some hold as a civilizing influence on centre-left politics, where, sadly, there is a dearth of defenders of the kind of principled approach to political power that liberal egalitarianism advocates. I remain enough of a rationalist to believe that it is both a necessary and desirable reason for retaining political thought in the university curriculum, in order that it can serve this role of contributing to the education of an active and humane citizenry.

Liberal egalitarianism both needs and deserves a regular restatement and defence – I aim to provide such a defence in this book. But what is liberal egalitarianism? To answer that question will take the rest of this book, which is itself merely a fraction of what would be required for a full philosophical and political defence. Nevertheless, before turning to that longer story I can identify some key features of liberal egalitarianism.

Whereas many commentators and philosophers continue to see liberalism as primarily about liberty, other liberal thinkers have claimed that the core value at the heart of liberalism is not liberty but rather equality. This point has been made most recently and powerfully by Ronald Dworkin, but it is a view widely shared amongst liberal political theorists, and as we shall see it is a view that has deep roots in the history of liberal egalitarianism.[7] But identifying equality as the core value of liberalism raises a number of problems and ambiguities. For many, equality suggests sameness and the denial of difference, and as such is not a value at all but is actually antithetical to liberalism. Many nineteenth-century liberals, for example, saw equality as a 'levelling system', where that levelling was always downwards and thus a denial of the difference, diversity and autonomy that confers value on human existence. Such liberals are anti-egalitarian, seeing the political emancipation offered by democratic movements as a threat to culture and civilization: this was certainly the view of both Von Humboldt and J. S. Mill in the nineteenth century.[8] This common perspective of the nineteenth century was also shared by many twentieth-century liberals such as Friedrich Hayek. Other philosophers, of a less conservative character, still concur with the view that equality is not really a value as such but rather a distributive relation, which might be attached to a host of different values.[9] As a distributive relation (what Joseph Raz calls a 'principle of closure') it can be shown to be anything but valuable by the application of a thought experiment which asks whether, in the distribution of bad things such as illnesses or disabilities, the application of equality as a distributive criterion makes things more or less valuable. Most people would argue that the equalization of circumstances by distributing disabilities is both absurd and repugnant.

In response to these challenges liberal egalitarians claim that equality is a complex of person-regarding values and relations. The core of this position is the fundamental ethical view, claiming that which is of most value is the human

person, and however we characterize that value it is something that is exemplified by all human persons – equally. All
human beings matter equally simply in virtue of their
common moral status as equal moral subjects. There are
numerous origins for this belief, both religious and humanis-
tic, but the core idea is neither confined to any of these
sources nor does it depend on the truth of any of these comprehensive moral, philosophical or theological perspectives.
What does matter is that the idea of equality of concern and
respect is both widely held and attractive to individuals and
groups beyond the confines of any particular system or
culture. Of course, merely agreeing that all persons should be
treated with equality of concern and respect does not answer
all questions. Not least, we are left with the question of what
sort of treatment ensures equality of concern and respect.
Liberal egalitarian philosophers and theorists differ in how
we should answer that question. However, it is no small
achievement to defend fundamental equality of status, as for
much of human history and in most parts of the world this
idea has been anything but the norm. Social status, race, eth-
nicity, gender, age, capacity for reason or education – indeed
almost any criterion of difference has been used to challenge
or deny equality of concern and respect. The contemporary
turn towards difference, partiality and group-based identity
brings with it the risk of overturning this precious and
precarious achievement, so it needs constant restatement as
well as defence. The vitality and urgency of this truth is as
important as its philosophical defence.

Most liberal egalitarians hesitate at offering any single and
conclusive defence of their core commitment. In this, they are
no doubt right to acknowledge that there is no single knock-
down argument in favour of equality of concern and respect.
That said, one must not infer from this fact that there are no
reasons for being an egalitarian that are more compelling
than the reasons we have for being anti-egalitarian. It is not
simply a matter of blind existential choice. While the philosophical arguments for equal moral status are precarious and
subject to critique, they are less dubious than the arguments
so far offered for the contrary position. All theological and
quasi-scientific arguments for natural hierarchy or group difference are more spurious still, and, what is more, they are

highly ineffective in persuading those whose status is being denied that they are less deserving of moral consideration than others, and ought to be discriminated against. In the end it has only ever been force and coercion that has sustained social relations of inequality. Although a pure regime of liberal equality exists nowhere at present, we know enough from the experience of more liberal and democratic states that they rely on less coercion and force, at least to the extent of persuading citizens that they are equally deserving of civil liberties, rights and welfare.

We can distinguish two components to the principles of liberal egalitarianism defended in this book. At the philosophical level there is the basic substantive value of equal personhood. At the political level are the principles which distribute the rights and economic resources necessary to protect equal personhood. Although guided by the former, political liberalism is mostly concerned with the shape of political principles that are guided by that basic philosophical commitment to equality.

It is the moral significance of the human person that is at the heart of liberal egalitarianism first and foremost. This makes liberalism an individualistic doctrine. Individualism is often seen as a problem in that it presupposes a false social ontology, by radically atomizing society and dissolving social bonds. Many versions of liberalism are indeed open to such criticisms, but it is not an essential feature of liberal egalitarian individualism that it must be 'atomistic'. Liberal egalitarianism is individualistic in an ethical or normative sense only. That means that in asserting the equal dignity of persons it attaches supreme ethical significance to the human person. This does not entail the denial of any particular social ontology and how persons may well find their identities in, or have their identities conferred by, group membership. It merely asserts that the sociological or social-psychological account of identity is not the last word on ethical or normative significance. Many critics of liberalism still dismiss it out of hand because of its apparent denial of social context and constitutive attachments to others that make up our individual identity. This criticism has been addressed extensively and rejected conclusively. No liberal egalitarian is required to follow Margaret Thatcher and claim that 'there is no such thing as society'. What liberals do claim is that no constitutive attachment, either to state, nation, family or cultural group, must trump the claims of individuals and their basic rights and status.

The equal status attached to all human persons has also often been thought to entail that liberals are primarily concerned with personal autonomy. Yet, whether liberal egalitarians must attach value to autonomy is a secondary matter and depends on how one fleshes out the commitment to equality of concern and respect. The reason that autonomy is often seen as the core liberal value is that it is supposed to be the best explanation of the idea of liberal rights and protections that are central to liberal egalitarians. Liberals undoubtedly cash-out the idea of equal moral status in terms of the distribution of a set of basic rights and titles. These consist of both civil and political rights and protections, as well as claims of economic resources and wealth. These form the subject matter of political liberalism, as we shall see in chapters 4 and 5. These rights constitute protected spheres that place the individual beyond the reach of the coercive claims of the state or society. Of course these protections are only ethical and not practical. Any regime that wants to discard the legitimate claims of individuals can do so. The only force underpinning such protections is moral and is wielded by public opinion, whether national or international. Sceptics often use this fact about rights (a fact which applies as much to legal as to political rights) as a basis for the claim that rights and civil liberties are not much use in the face of the real world of political power and coercion. It is also common to dismiss the culture of rights as an inconvenience that interferes with the real demands of politics. While one can overstate the significance of rights, as sometimes happens in American political theory, we should not lose sight of the power of rights claims as normative reasons, nor should we lose sight of the power of reasons in motivating or restraining political actions.

The civil and political rights at the heart of liberal egalitarianism provide individuals with a morally protected sphere, and it is this that is seen to involve the idea of autonomy. Within this sphere individuals have final discretion about moral, political and religious issues and life choices. This seems to suggest that it is individual choice and endorsement that matters most in determining the authority of any moral viewpoint. Undoubtedly, liberal egalitarians do attach significance to choice or endorsement of moral viewpoints, but it is not obvious that this entails a commitment by them to any strong doctrine of autonomy as the basic value of liberal egalitarianism. If it is merely the case that respect for persons is an autonomy-regarding view because liberals attach value to endorsement and choice, then there is not much to the claim about autonomy and liberal egalitarians might well concede it. However, theorists who attach value to autonomy, especially those in the Kantian tradition, generally use the idea of autonomous choice as self-legislation. This rather complex idea takes us back into the metaphysics of free will and the idea of positive freedom, which we will consider in chapter 4. Strong autonomy theories focus on the idea of the individual's will, so that individuals can be seen as non-autonomous if they make choices of the wrong sort. Liberal egalitarians tend to respect choices, as long as they are not the subject of direct external political coercion and are made within the sphere of an individual's personal discretion. The distinction turns on the role of choice. Strong autonomy theories like those of Kant and Rousseau focus on the kinds of choices made; weak autonomy of theories focus on choice within one's set of rights and liberties, rather than its character. Liberal egalitarians are certainly not committed to autonomy in this stronger sense, although some do endorse such a philosophical position. As the use of the concept of autonomy involves some slippage between these two senses, it is helpful to reserve it for the strong, positive freedom thesis, and instead focus on equal rights and opportunities as being at the heart of political liberalism. Equality of concern and respect is certainly consistent with individuals making life choices or endorsing moral viewpoints that attach little or no significance to autonomy as the source of morality. Instead liberal egalitarianism is concerned with equality as a political value that is concerned with the regulation of legitimate coercion. The imposition of certain moral, religious or political views on individuals by the coercive power of the political community is to deny the equal status of individuals; in that sense it is a denial of equality or concern and respect, and it is that alone which makes it wrong. Thus civil and political rights set the boundaries to the limits of legitimate coercion by the state or wider society and provide similar boundaries to personal discretion. Within that sphere of personal discretion, individuals have, effectively, a right to do wrong.[10] It needs to be stressed here that this right to do wrong follows for the important reason that liberal egalitarianism does not take the view that there are no objective moral values and therefore that individual choices are the sole determinant of what we call values.[11] Some liberals are sceptics and take precisely this view, but it is not necessary that all *must* do so. Liberal egalitarianism, as a political doctrine, is about the legitimate use of coercion or political power, and one can reasonably argue that while some choices are morally wrong or personally harmful, it is not appropriate that they be subject to political coercion or force. Thus it can genuinely be the case that individuals enjoying equal concern and respect can have a right to harm themselves or hold beliefs and values that are false or repugnant to others. This is one of the more demanding features of a liberal egalitarian view and one that is easiest to drop in the face of majority opinion, but in the end it is this view which sustains a humane and civil political community. It is also this view that underpins political liberalism, as it confines the scope of liberal values to the political realm where they underpin fair terms of social cooperation. It is not the goal of liberal politics to foster human perfection or to make men moral.

Another important feature of the liberal egalitarian view about rights and civil liberties is that it is not subject to the political charge that it places too much emphasis on rights and not enough on responsibilities. 'No rights without responsibilities' is a platitude trumpeted by New Labour in Britain, by apostles of the Third Way such as Blair, and former President Clinton in the US, as well as communitarians on both sides of the Atlantic, and many social democrats. Yet, like all platitudes, it ignores the central truth of the liberal egalitarian's understanding of rights.

Liberal egalitarians, unlike libertarians such as the late Robert Nozick, are not committed to the idea that individuals have a narrow set of pre-political rights which place 'side-constraints' on human interaction, this being the end of the matter. Instead, liberal egalitarians have always argued that equality of concern and respect brings with it not only rights as civil protections, but also positive rights to economic justice. Both sets of rights create strong obligations and duties on individuals to contribute their fair share to social justice and the worst-off in society. Different liberal egalitarians give weaker or stronger accounts of the demands of these obligations, duties and responsibilities, but it is simply ignorance to argue that liberals are only concerned about rights and not about responsibilities. The two concepts, as just about every theorist of rights since Jeremy Bentham has acknowledged, always go hand in hand. The issue between different liberal egalitarians is what kind of rights and what kind of responsibilities?

To sum up the basic commitments of the egalitarian political liberalism that will be the focus in this book, we can identify four components, the first two of which refer to its philosophical basis and the second two to its political claims:

1 All individuals are of equal and ultimate moral value.
2 This individualism is ethical and not sociological or psychological.
3 Equality of concern and respect is cashed-out in terms of a set of basic rights, civil liberties and economic entitlements. These rights entail accompanying responsibilities and duties.
4 Ethical individualism and equality of concern and respect does not entail moral scepticism about objective values. It is instead concerned with the moral limitation of coercion or political power.

The early chapters of the book will provide an account of the philosophical origins of liberal egalitarianism and its more recent development as a political theory. The remainder of the book is concerned with its defence against four strands of contemporary criticism. These criticisms overlap, but can be distinguished as those forming an attack on the theoretical foundations of liberal egalitarianism, and those consisting of three political criticisms of liberalism. Defending political liberalism against these three political challenges is as important as defending political liberalism's philosophical credentials. This is so because liberal theorists are not merely engaged in a philosophical exercise but are concerned to connect their theories with the real world of politics. If the political objections hold then the philosophical task, whether completely or partly successful, risks being potentially redundant. That said, the philosophical and political criticism of liberalism is interconnected. The four strands of criticism addressed in the last three chapters are as follows:

1   That political liberalism misunderstands the nature and demands of politics. In the form in which this criticism is advanced by, amongst others, Glen Newey,[12] liberal egalitarianism is a profoundly anti-political doctrine that threatens to displace the demands of politics and to subordinate them to the privileged role of the political philosopher.

2   The second issue turns to the philosophical claims underpinning liberalism. In particular we shall address what I have called the ethnocentric objection, which is not simply that liberalism is based on a false conception of neutrality, but that it posits a set of narrow and culturally specific political prejudices as universal values and principles. This objection underpins both communitarianism and its most common contemporary variant in multiculturalism, with its challenge to liberalism as a disguised version of cultural imperialism. My task in this chapter will not be a full philosophical defence of liberalism, but I will challenge the idea that the conception of philosophical justification that underpins liberalism rests on a disguised politics of cultural imperialism.

I then turn to two claims about liberal political theory and its connection to the state.

3   The first of these claims is raised by multiculturalists and group rights theorists. Here I am not simply concerned with the question of whether egalitarians can take culture seriously, rather I address the more fundamental claim advanced by the likes of Bhikhu Parekh[13] that liberal egalitarians have a narrowly state-centred view of

politics. This criticism reflects a similar claim advanced by Quentin Skinner and James Tully,[14] to the effect that modern liberalism is constrained by the conception of the modern juridical state which underlies it, and that consequently it cannot take seriously the claims of any groups or associations between the individual and the state.

4 The second of these criticisms addresses the potential redundancy of liberal egalitarianism as a consequence of globalization and the retreat of the state. This view has been advanced recently by David Held and Peter Singer,[15] who both argue that the aspirations of liberal egalitarianism are best sought by thinking beyond the boundaries of liberalism in the direction of a cosmopolitan conception of political association.

In the last three chapters I will set out the basic challenge and show that liberalism is either immune to it, or can withstand it. Each chapter will identify the most contemporary and therefore pressing of these persistent criticisms. Obviously, in a short book like this not all the nuances of criticism can be accommodated, but the basic outlines of a liberal response to this persistent wave of criticism can be identified. As pointed out earlier, my main concern is to reiterate the significance and vitality of liberal egalitarianism. If this task is successful, it is up to students and readers to pursue these issues in more detail with the great contemporary liberal egalitarian thinkers. Those who, for perfectly understandable reasons, do not wish to devote themselves to political theory or the history of thought can still derive something of value from the restatement of the liberal egalitarian viewpoint. John Stuart Mill, in his defence of freedom of speech in *On Liberty*, argues for the significance of negative criticism of even true beliefs as a necessary means of maintaining their vitality and significance among the public.[16] Political theory, in the modern university, continues that important source of intellectual training through negative criticism. Indeed, most political theory teaching takes the form of finding 'the three things wrong with Plato's *Republic*, Hegel's *Philosophy of Right* or Rawls' *A Theory of Justice*.' In both the anglophone and continental traditions, constructive theorizing is the exception rather than the norm. There is nothing wrong with this; negative criticism is important for precisely the sort of reasons that Mill suggests, and constructive theory is extraordinarily difficult even for the brightest minds. Yet, just as there is a place for negative criticism and for the rare flashes of constructive theory, there is also a role for positive restatement as part of the same process that Mill identifies. On its own, negative criticism, though supremely important, can have the corrosive tendency towards total scepticism. For the scholar, intellectual or philosopher there are no better reasons for one political view than any other view. Many anti-rationalists influenced by Michael Oakeshott tend to take this sceptical view, although I do not believe that it was Oakeshott's view. This kind of sceptical view is not only wrong, it is also dangerous as it does have an effect on our political culture. To counter it we need positive restatements and defences of liberal egalitarianism, just as much as we need criticism of and challenges to its more hubristic claims. What makes this book a modest defence of liberalism is that I do not propose to silence critics of liberal egalitarianism. What I do intend to show is that the critics do not necessarily have the last word.

2
The Sources of Liberal Equality

Equality, in the sense used by liberal egalitarians to underpin political liberalism, is a peculiarly modern value. Although the roots of equal concern and respect can be found in pre-modern and classical theological and philosophical world views, the idea of equality as a distinct value is a modern development, as is the related connection between personal inviolability and equality. Pre-modern world views such as those of Plato, Cicero or St Augustine have little place for equality as a distinct value. Thus, while one could attempt to trace the roots of liberal egalitarianism in Jewish, Christian or even Islamic theodicies, as well as in the philosophy of Aristotle, the most important sources of liberal egalitarianism are to be found in modern European thought – by which I mean the post-Reformation period. This fact is often taken to be a problem for liberalism as it is supposed to limit its scope and authority – I deal with the criticism in detail later in chapter 7. In the early modern period the idea of the modern individual emerged as a distinct bearer of ethical significance, most commonly as a result of protestant accounts of justification. Within a very short time one sees this idea of the individual permeate many different aspects of life, not just the religious. This core idea of ethical individualism is central to the subsequent development of the European Enlightenment, in which it is progressively distanced from the direct need for theological justification. In the course of this chapter

I will provide an account of the development of this idea of ethical individualism as it is explored in the contractualist and utilitarian traditions, from which many of our contemporary ideas concerning liberal equality are derived.[1] As this section is concerned with the sources of liberal egalitarianism's central ethical idea, the argument will focus on a number of important philosophers and abstract philosophical arguments. This should not lead one to assume that the philosophical roots of liberal ideas are all that is necessary in order to arrive at egalitarian political liberalism. That said, the development of contractualism is important in that it provides the philosophical language and arguments through which liberal egalitarians explain their core ethical commitment.

In providing an account of the origins of the liberal egalitarian position, I do not propose to offer a full theory of the history of liberal ideas. As I have already indicated I am sceptical about the possibility of such a history. Liberalism is simply too complex an ideological, philosophical and sociological concept to be captured by a single history of manageable proportions. However, the main reason for my selective historical narrative is that I am working backwards from the present – in terms of a contemporary political theory – to identify sources for, rather than causes of, this contemporary perspective. This gives my 'history' the kind of whiggish character many contemporary historians of political thought are inclined to object to, because it seems to assert the causal necessity of present political relationships. It is not my purpose to assert any such simplistic causal story. The rise of liberal egalitarianism is far from inevitable and this holds true for the rise of the modern state. That said, like the state, the idea of liberal egalitarianism was constructed from some philosophical and ideological resources, and it is those which I wish to outline. Furthermore, the liberal egalitarian theory is composed of a variety of distinct values, which only become a version of liberalism when combined with each other. There are also sources of liberal egalitarian ideas, such as utilitarianism, which in its subsequent development has been thought of as inimical to, rather than supportive of, the liberal egalitarian position. This is despite the acknowledged fact that as a political and ideological movement utilitarianism did much to contribute to the emergence of liberal ideas.

Before turning to this brief history and analysis of the emergence of a liberal conception of equality, and its opposition to that derived from utilitarianism, it might be useful to provide a few simple definitions. The first form of contract theory we will consider can be described as a mutual advantage theory. The agreements of *mutual advantage* theories are ones in which all the parties recognize a benefit or advantage. They do *not*, however, claim that we must all benefit equally. I can, for example, agree to a distribution of property as being to my advantage, even if you have more than me, because at least under this distribution I have more than I might have had under a different system. The next important distinction is between *impartiality* theories and *impersonality* theories. Both perspectives share something in common, but political theorists like to draw an important distinction between the two concepts. *Impartiality* involves not favouring one person over another. As such, it is claimed to be both egalitarian (treating everyone equally) and person-respecting, in that it respects the separateness of persons as being each equally a beneficiary of a distribution. *Impersonality* is claimed to be a basis of fair distribution because it makes no reference to any particular person. In this way, it is claimed it can provide a criterion of fair distribution which does not take account of the identities of beneficiaries of the distribution. Consequently it can result in a disproportionate distribution of resources between persons. The lack of any reference to a particular person means it cannot provide a reason for securing each particular person with a share of the benefit.

Central to the development of the egalitarian liberalism I wish to defend in this book is the idea of impartiality. Equality of concern and respect is not reducible to the idea of impartiality, but impartiality remains an important feature of the liberal concept of equality. In exploring this connection between impartiality and equality of concern and respect we need to range over the contractualist and utilitarian traditions. The idea of impartiality involves not giving anyone more than their share and is central to understanding concepts such as justice and fairness. In its most simple form it involves not giving special consideration or attention to some at the expense of others. It is often described as a procedural virtue; hence its connection with legal justice and constitutional ideas of political rule as an ordered procedure for distributing the collective coercive power of a political community. In contemporary political philosophy it is inextricably linked to the recent resurgence of interest in the social contract tradition and the associated discourse of distributive justice.[2] However, the idea is not the peculiar property of contractualist thinking as it is also central to the ideal of the impartial spectator, found in thinkers as diverse as Adam Smith in the eighteenth century and contemporary utilitarians, such as the late R. M. Hare.[3] It is also central to the development of constructivist ethical theories derived from the ideas of Immanuel Kant.[4] In all of these accounts, whatever their many significant differences, the ideal of impartiality is deployed as a procedural guarantee of a decision or norm being reasonable. Reasonableness is the 'good' which justifies a norm, policy or action, but it is impartiality which provides the criterion or test of reasonableness, where reasonableness involves not merely having a first-person 'reason for me' but rather a third-person 'reason for all'. As such, the significance of impartiality is most clearly manifest in the social contract tradition which sees the tasks of moral or political philosophy as discontinuous – the provision of public reasons that limit the exercise of subjective freedom and also the coercive power of the state or polity. (I use the idea of the polity to refer to any form of political association. The state is merely one type of polity that has emerged at a particular point in history.) That is not to deny the ideal of impartiality in pre-modern ethical and political theories, but it is to acknowledge that impartiality has a particular role in our understanding of morality as a peculiar institution of rules governing interpersonal interaction that eliminates arbitrariness, self-preference, or privileging special attachments. In the same way political theories of the modern constitutional state set boundaries to the interaction of agents within the body politic, whether these be individuals, rulers, groups or corporations.

The parallel between moral reasoning and political justification is most clearly seen in the case of the contract tradition, going back at least to the work of the English philosopher Thomas Hobbes (1588–1679). Hobbes famously used the idea of an agreement to explain the origins of political authority and our subjection to the sovereign. He presents an account of pre-social individuals living in a state of nature. That is, of people with desires and wants before the existence of either society or, more importantly, political community. With no social attachments, rules or authoritative moral principles, individuals enjoy unlimited subjective right – that is, liberty unconstrained by anything, including the similar liberty of others. In this natural condition each person has a subjective right to everything, even the life and body of others. The consequence of this is constant war. The burden of this war of all against all provides each person with a reason to alienate or transfer her subjective right to authorize a single sovereign power. This sovereign political power then imposes laws that regulate conduct and create rights, obligations and duties on all people equally. Hobbes' dark vision of a world without order, and of the artificial character of political society, moral principles and law, has been hugely influential on subsequent theorists of the state and political power. Within this complex argument the idea of impartiality plays a weak and minor role, applying only to the recognition that such an agreement to alienate one's liberty or subjective right would take place 'when others are so [willing] to lay down this right to all things; and be contented with so much liberty against other men, as he would allow other men against himselfe'.[5] That said, Hobbes' argument does require that, at least at this point, each individual should attach equal weight to the claims of all others, in order to explain the emergence and authority of the political sovereign. Unless each can recognize that each person desires peace and will forego her immediate advantage, Hobbes' argument does not get off the ground and consequently there is no escape from the state of nature. In so arguing Hobbes provides a connection, albeit weak, between the idea of impartiality and equality that is central to the subsequent development of contractarian political and constitutional thinking. The idea of equality in Hobbes is rooted in the idea of the natural equality of power. By this, Hobbes means to imply that each person in the state of nature is in fact equal in terms of power for the simple reason that physical strength can be trumped by superior guile and cunning, and that even the most powerful are vulnerable in their sleep. How plausible this assumption is remains an open question. What is important for Hobbes is that his account of equality is empirical and descriptive, and not normative, as it is prior to the artificial creation of any moral norms. Hobbesian natural equality translates into potentially equal bargaining power, thus guaranteeing a free and fair outcome and hence one which all rational individuals could be taken to endorse.

The issue of equal bargaining power has remained a deeply controversial idea right into contemporary contractualist thinking and it underpins the persistent disagreement between what are called *mutual advantage* and *impartialist* variants of social contract thinking.[6] Part of the reason for this is the hopelessly implausible idea that for all practical purposes every individual enjoys equality of power. This was clearly Hobbes' view, but equally clearly it is implausible, especially in contemporary arguments, which are not simply concerned with the authorization of sovereign political power but with the justification of moral principles or distributive justice. In the most morally pressing cases where we might be considering the just claims of the absolutely worse off, such as the physically disabled, elderly and infirm and dependent children, to conceive of them as all having equal bargaining power is patently false. If individuals do not enjoy equality of bargaining power then contractualist arguments can fail to deliver fairness, as unequal bargainers will be able to impose terms that reflect their own positional advantage and luck. As we shall see, the desire to eradicate the effects of luck on the distribution of rights, opportunities and life chances is central to the egalitarian liberal. Contemporary *mutual advantage* contract theorists such as David Gauthier are prepared to live with the austere conclusions of this criticism, by arguing that any contract must include only those who contribute to the benefits of social cooperation, thus excluding most of the problematic cases I referred to above. Hobbes has little or nothing to say on what contemporary theorists describe as distributive justice, and most commentators tend to see him as, at best, only a very peculiar kind of liberal.[7] That said, Hobbes provides a good account of some of the central building blocks of the liberal egalitarian viewpoint, and a starting point for their development. With Hobbes, we see the idea of individuality and equal status (of a peculiar kind) as the basic building block of moral and political justification. And furthermore a conception of justification that must ignore the particularities of individual wants, aspirations and relationships to other people.

Hobbesian 'mutual advantage' contractarianism is not the only direction in which contractarian thinking developed: indeed until the twentieth century this aspect of Hobbes' argument soon fell into relative obscurity. The direction in which contract theory developed after Hobbes was one that he explicitly rejected. Contract theory became associated almost exclusively with consent theory. The main figure with whom this turn in the direction of contract theory is most closely associated is John Locke (1632–1704). Much contemporary scholarship has been concerned to situate Locke within the particularities of seventeenth-century religious, philosophical and political debates, and to deny his relevance for theorizing modern egalitarian liberalism.[8] Yet Locke's theories contain powerful statements of some of the basic building blocks of liberal egalitarianism. This is most clearly seen in his account of the social contract, and his development of a consent theory of political association on its basis. In this way the social contract is used to explain the origin of political (but not civil) society and its continual legitimacy. Locke is concerned to avoid the political 'absolutism' of arguments such as those of Hobbes, and his contract is not designed to provide a foundation for basic moral norms. This is not to assert that Locke is directly responding to Hobbes, but it is to claim that Locke's alternative understanding of the nature and limits of political society, based on a prior recognition of the equal moral status of all mankind, is a direct repudiation of the idea that the natural or basic equality of all human beings entails political absolutism. Locke's argument in the second volume of *Two Treatises of Government*[9] is a purely political variant of contractualism, as it employs a pre-political moral norm to distribute basic rights to life, liberty and property, rather than using the agreement itself to ground the moral norm. For Hobbes, remember that all moral and political norms are secondary and therefore derived from the absolute sovereign: consequently sovereign political power knows no limit. For Locke, on the other hand, political power is always subject to a prior moral norm of equality of right, which places constraints upon what government can legitimately do without violating those rights. This norm embodies a form of *moral* equality that constrains and negates the practical significance of any material or physical inequalities. Consequently, Locke's contractarian theory employs a more substantive conception of equality than does Hobbes'. For Locke, equality is moral equality and therefore the basis of a claim to equal concern and respect, at least with respect to a set of basic rights. What Locke's contractarianism does not directly provide is a justification for the basic norm of moral recognition, or why we should recognize and treat others as moral equals with the same status and claims as ourselves. It is important to provide some account of their origins if the ideas of impartiality and fundamental equality are to have some prescriptive or obligation-creating force. The idea of the social contract and the related concept of consent is clearly dependent on the prior authority of fundamental equality. A failure to support that premise does appear to weaken his egalitarian theory. Furthermore, as we have seen, that norm of basic equality must be ethical and not merely empirical, as Hobbes suggests. Today, perhaps we are more inclined to live with the consequences of the incompleteness of an egalitarian theory, as in our democratic cultures some conception of equality is taken for granted by all but racists, bigots and homophobes. For Locke, the situation was rather different, hence his sustained (and, to a twenty-first-century audience, obsessive) need to refute the scriptural arguments of Sir Robert Filmer against natural and fundamental equality and in favour of natural hierarchy. To provide this defence of fundamental moral equality Locke turns to a more traditional, and theologically sanctioned, conception of natural law to provide the basis for his moral theory. However, his justification of this basic moral norm is both weak and controverisal in the face of reasonable disagreement (even amongst Christians) about the nature, scope and epistemological status of the law of nature. Indeed, many are inclined to think that Locke's argument is actually undermined by the empirical psychology that he developed in *An Essay Concerning Human Understanding*.[10] Although

Locke's argument fails to provide a non-question-begging justification for this norm of equality (a basic right to equal freedom), he provides us with a further insight into certain central building blocks of egalitarian liberalism, such as impartiality, consent or endorsement and the irreducible ethical significance of the person. Locke combines these ideas into a political theory of consent and political obligation, but this idea of consent can be extended beyond the confines of such a narrow political purpose. As contract and consent theories of political obligation came under increasing criticism during the eighteenth century, from David Hume, Edmund Burke and Jeremy Bentham, the ideas of reasonable consent, endorsement or agreement were being taken up by other later contract theorists to provide an account of the authority of moral norms.[11] We can see this transformation most clearly in the case of Immanuel Kant. Whether Kant is properly a contract theorist is a matter of serious scholarly debate, with many important scholars such as Onora O'Neill denying this claim. Kant certainly does not have a consent theory of political obligation such as we saw in Locke, nor does he endorse the kind of mutual advantage alienation contract that we find in Hobbes. That said, Kant's reworking of elements of contract arguments has had a huge influence on the subsequent development of contract theory, particularly in the development of impartialist contractualisms in the last four decades. For our purposes, it is sufficient that later thinkers have interpreted Kant as a contractualist; as such he has had a profound influence on the development of contractualist variants of liberalism.

Kant's argument is only equivocally contractualist because he does not use the idea of an agreement or bargain to explain the emergence of norms. Norms, whether moral or municipal, have a variety of sources, such as the commands of the king, the will of God or the conventional practices of a particular city, yet what matters for Kant is their authority or 'normativity', not their source. Neither history and culture, nor individual and group interest, have any bearing on the authority of laws and norms, and hence their ability to generate obligations and duties. The legitimacy of laws and moral norms is guaranteed, so long as those norms are such that rational men could have consented to them as the outcome of a hypothetical agreement. Yet, whereas this consent had to be actual in the Lockean case, through express agreements or through certain actions which embody tacit consent, Kant's ideal of rational consent is very different. His process of rational consent is simply the recognition of the reasonableness of the moral law, and, therefore, while it can be described as rational consent it does not mean inter-personal agreement. (For many, this is why Kant is not a con-tractualist.) In making this argument Kant frees the contract tradition from its origins in voluntarism – expressions of will rather than reason. Instead the contract is not an example of a choice, even a hypothetical one; rather, it becomes a device for describing how we recognize the obligation-creating force of authoritative reasons. It does not matter whether these reasons originate in the will of the monarch whose authority is derived from conquest or birth, or from a republican con-stitution. What matters, is that the laws could be the subject of the consent of reasonable men. Thus, the contract device becomes for Kant a purely hypothetical procedure for deter-mining the legitimacy or genuineness of putative moral and political norms, dispensing with the need for accounts of the state of nature.

Legitimate laws are those that could be characterized as resulting from a hypothetical agreement between reasonable men. But what did Kant mean by 'reasonable' in this context? He certainly did not mean men who wish to maximize their individual or collective advantage. At the very least, it is pre-cisely this idea that morality must be reducible to advantage that Kant wanted to dispense with in his distinction between moral norms as categorical imperatives rather than hypo-thetical imperatives. Instead, the idea of reasonableness is closely connected to the ideal of impartiality and equality of recognition, so that a reasonable agreement would be one that did not depend upon advantage, inequality or self-preference, but could be justified to anyone, whatever their social position. Moral justification for Kant takes the form of requiring reasonable consent, provided that reason-ableness is defined not in terms of advantage but rather as impartiality based upon the rational will.

The real significance, for us, of Kant's transformation of the social contract tradition is to be found in his model of proceduralism as the appropriate form of moral and political justification. Moral and political norms are authorized and legitimized as they emerge from a certain kind of procedure. For Kant this procedure is the form of individual practical reasoning and not the result of an interpersonal bargain or agreement. It is a thought process that any individual can go through on their own as long as they adopt the perspective of impartiality, through being able to universalize their moral maxims, so that they could have the form of law, as categorical imperatives. The idea of the categorical imperative that Kant develops in his *Groundwork of the Metaphysics of Morals*, is often misunderstood as being vacuous. Yet it is important to understand that Kant intends it as a test for the authority of maxims and not as an action-guiding rule itself. Kant's theory is intended to apply to the foundations of all moral norms; as such its scope is very broad and that renders it controversial, particularly amongst those who regard morality as being less about principle and more about virtue and character. Kant's account of the authority of moral norms presupposes a particular view about what the practice or institutional structure of morality is.[12] As this account is supposed to provide a justification for our most basic moral commitments, it is connected with a complex philosophical anthropology, explaining how it is that moral agency is possible and what kind of agent a moral agent must be. In this way, Kant hoped to avoid finding himself in the same situation as Locke, in having to retreat to a traditional theological conception of natural law as the basis for equal recognition and impartial treatment. His arguments raise important issues and they still preoccupy critical and sympathetic scholars.

That said, it is by no means certain that Kant's answer to fundamental questions about freedom and agency or moral subjectivity are essential to the application and development of his ideas of impartial justification and equal recognition. If we look at the development of modern contractualist arguments we find that many who derive insights from Kant about the nature and scope of moral norms combine this with a naturalistic account of moral motivation. Such a theory does not reduce all human agency to a crude empirical account of desire satisfaction, such as we find in Hobbes or with utilitarians such as Bentham. Nevertheless, it does make the account of motivation and agency conditional on what we know about human psychology. To avoid being drawn into complex discussions about the nature of the self and the conditions of human agency and moral motivation, contemporary contractarians such as T. M. Scanlon and Brian Barry appeal to the fact of an agreement motive. That is, both claim that, as long as there is a motive to seek reasonable agreement or to act morally, we have enough psychology to allow us to get on with the issue of characterizing the claims of morality or liberal justice.[13] The evidence for this motive is provided by the fact that people do both defend and disagree about the scope of obligations to others. How widespread such a motive is and whether it is sufficiently overriding, remain important questions, given that it would not do any real work if it always gave way to the egoistic motives of self-preference. Nevertheless, its existence as demonstrated by the practice of moral justification means that we do not necessarily need to provide a full moral psychology or metaphysic of the person before we can engage in thinking about moral and political justification. This fact is extremely important given the aspiration of political liberalism to make only weak demands of controversial philosophical and ethical theories and perspectives.

Clearly, the foundation or basis of our commitment to equal concern and respect is not a trivial matter, as Jeremy Waldron reminds us in his discussion of Locke. But even if we do not follow Kant's metaphysics of the person, we can derive much from the way in which Kant's proceduralism models some ideas of equal treatment in the most fundamental respects of reason-giving as a condition of imposing or recognizing obligations. It is for this reason that contractualism has proved so attractive to many liberal and democratic thinkers in the twentieth century. This is not merely fortuitous because Kant's normative proceduralism also reflects a parallel political ideal of constitutionalism as a procedure that sets out how legitimate political decisions can be made, and what sort of decisions they can be. He can be seen to generalize the idea of a fair constitutional procedure into a basic method for practical deliberation. This move is often regarded as making individual practical deliberation hope-

lessly demanding, as in most instances of practical deliberation we cannot make genuinely impartial judgements that
treat others as equals. Kant did have a rigorous account of
the demands of morality, but most contemporary contractualist theories have been concerned with limiting the demands
of impartiality in individual practical reasoning and developing the idea of proceduralism as a political theory, applying
to issues such as distributive justice.

Kant's contribution to the contractualist tradition provides
an important inspiration for thinking about the nature of a
fair procedure for political decision-making. Yet this seems
to suggest that what is most important is simply what might
be called constitutional essentials, that is the distribution of
civil and political rights. But this is not all there is to liberal
egalitarianism. Indeed, in the last few decades attention
has turned more towards issues of material equality and
resources, and away from merely specifying a set of civil
and political rights. Interestingly, the concern for equality of
circumstances has its roots as much in the utilitarian tradition as it does in contractualism.

It is one of the great ironies of modern political philosophy that the utilitarian tradition, which is so important a
contributor to the growth and development of liberal
ideas, should now be seen as almost a shorthand for anti-
liberalism. This is a turn of events that still remains a puzzle
to many liberal-minded utilitarians. Historically, the term
'liberal' was introduced into English as a term of abuse,
applied to the godless doctrines of utilitarians such as Jeremy
Bentham in the early nineteenth century. And one of the
greatest figures in the liberal pantheon, who must stand as an
equal to John Locke and Immanuel Kant, is John Stuart Mill,
perhaps the most significant utilitarian philosopher of all. The
utilitarian tradition has complex roots in seventeenth- and
eighteenth-century moral theory, but its first unequivocal
advocate and defender was the English philosopher Jeremy
Bentham (1748–1832). Bentham is credited with populariz-
ing the idea that the criterion for judging actions and
principles as morally obligatory is whether doing so would
maximize the greatest happiness of the greatest number.
Thus, whether we have rights, duties, or obligations depends
upon whether these maximize pleasure and minimize pain,

which Bentham took as the meaning of happiness. Actions are only right if they maximize the greatest happiness of the greatest number even if the law says otherwise.[14] That eighteenth-century law, so often, did say otherwise, was for Bentham a reason for its overhaul and reform.

Bentham and subsequent utilitarians such as John Stuart Mill were not only philosophical reformers, but were also political and legal reformers. Both advocated the extension of political rights, the reform of the constitution, the abolition of so-called 'harmless' offences in the law and widespread social and economic reforms. In so far as early utilitarians such as Bentham and Mill were radical reformers, they have much in common with contemporary liberal egalitarians, perhaps more than with the likes of Kant or John Locke, who had very conservative views about the scope of rights to private property. Whereas Locke and Kant give an account of private property rights that constrains state actions to bring about a more equal distribution of resources, utilitarians are more amenable to the idea that the distribution of resources and economic power should be constructed (and if necessary reconstructed) to maximize happiness or welfare. In this way, the major utilitarian theorists Bentham and Mill open up the possibility of social justice with respect to economic goods and powers as an implication of equal concern and respect. If individuals are to enjoy equality of concern and respect then they cannot be subject to poverty and disadvantage just because of an accident of history, or their inability to acquire adequate resources through the market mechanism. Contemporary liberal egalitarians develop these ideas at great length and in directions that neither Bentham nor Mill might have endorsed. Bentham saw the equalization of incomes as of only marginal significance and was more concerned with an equal right to basic subsistence. John Stuart Mill took varying views on the issue of social justice, from an early liberal position close to that of Bentham, to an interest in socialism under the influence of his wife Harriet Taylor, towards the end of his life. Either way, neither thought that equal treatment consisted solely in the distribution of equal civil and political rights, a position that was itself far from universally held in the nineteenth century. The rejection of a narrow formal equality before the law, in favour of a thicker conception of social and political equality as an essential corrective to the narrow libertarian strand of Lockean and Kantian contractualism, is central to the emergence of liberal egalitarian ideas in the twentieth century. It is important to remember this when evaluating the sources of liberal equality. That said, while the utilitarians, such as Bentham and Mill, give a corrective to the narrow formalism of contractualist rights, they do so with a theory that makes the pursuit of liberalism's central commitment, the equal concern and respect of all individuals, a contingent matter. This can be seen clearly if we look at the ideal of impartiality and equality that underlies utilitarianism.

The ideal of impartiality is not the peculiar prerogative of the contractualist tradition. One important alternative strand of such thinking is the impartial spectator theories deployed by utilitarians but derived from Adam Smith's *The Theory of Moral Sentiments*.[15] Smith used the idea of an impartial spectator to provide a test of the propriety of sympathetic responses to the character of others. The impartial spectator does not over-sympathize or attach undue weight to the feelings of some persons or groups over those of others. By establishing this distance in judgement the spectator provides an ideal standard for making moral judgements. It is a feature of moral judgements for Smith that they are not merely a reflection of individual interest and advantage. Again the central idea, similar to that found in Kant's contractarian universalizability test, is that the moral point of view is the impartial point of view free from immediate passions, private interests and partiality. Although Smith was not a utilitarian in any uncontroversial sense, this idea of an impartial spectator has been taken up by the utilitarian tradition as a device for balancing the preferences or interests of those covered by a utility calculation. It should be pointed out that it was not a device adopted by the two most important classical utilitarians, Jeremy Bentham and John Stuart Mill, however much it has come to be associated with the utilitarian tradition. John Rawls criticizes the idea of an impartial spectator as one of the structural inadequacies of utilitarian practical reasoning in his *A Theory of Justice*, whereas R. M. Hare, perhaps the most significant contemporary defender of utilitarianism, has deployed the idea through his model of 'critical' moral thinking.[16] One important way in which this method of impartialist thinking differs from that which derives from the contractarian tradition is that it translates the idea of impartiality into impersonality. This is because of the way in which utilitarian impartial spectator theories interpret the idea of equality of concern. As with contractarianism, utilitarianism deploys a notion of equality of concern. However, where for the contractarian this entails some notion of respect for the separateness of persons, for the utilitarian equality is satisfied by 'Bentham's dictum' 'that everyone is to count for one, no body for more than one'.[17] 'Bentham's dictum' is generally interpreted to imply that all preferences count once in a utility calculation. This attaches a formal equality of weight to each person's preference. When this idea is applied to the person of the impartial spectator it has the effect of creating impersonality rather than impartiality, as the object of value is an individual 'want' or 'preference' and not a person whose interest is concerned. Why this is problematic is that while it makes sense at the level of individual decision-making to sacrifice some present satisfaction in order to increase future welfare, when this ideal is applied to interpersonal decision-making, it has the effect of sacrificing the interests of some to those of the majority. In this way utilitarianism's theory of value, coupled with its conception of equality, creates impersonality out of impartiality. Many contemporary political philosophers reject this aspect of utilitarianism because it weakens the idea of person-regarding constraints on practical decision-making. If what is ultimately good is pleasurable states of affairs or satisfied wants, then the aggregate of these things will be most good and therefore what agents should pursue. This is so, whether these be private individuals, legislators or majorities of the voting public and even when these aggregates cause harm to other individuals or groups. While all public decision-making involves discounting the interests of some individuals against the interest of others, there must be constraints on how far this process can go and on what issues such sacrifices are acceptable. Is it, for example, acceptable to sacrifice the interests of ethnic minorities to improve the welfare of the majority, or to tolerate the punishment of the innocent in order to achieve zero-tolerance of crimes like burglary? The problem with utilitarianism is not simply that its conception of value and its conception of equality differ from that of contractualism. It is also that its account of impartiality, while acknowledging the need to stand back from one's self-interest and private commitments, fails to acknowledge the important idea of the separateness of persons. Here the conception of equality underlying the ideal of impartiality is itself person-regarding, and not merely utility- or want-regarding. This impartialist perspective brings with it the idea of person-regarding constraints on practical deliberation in the same way that the ideal of constitutionalism brings with it civil and political rights that constrain the exercise of majority and factional political power. The central issue for contemporary theorists of liberalism is to combine the concern for social justice that is derived from the utilitarian tradition with the person-regarding protections built into the contractualist model of political society. Modern liberal egalitarians are inspired by the legacy of early liberal utilitarians as much as by early contractarians. Yet the contractualist framework remains more attractive than the idea of a utility calculation, because it is premised upon the idea of the fundamental equal claim of all individuals as distinct persons, not merely to be counted, but to be treated with the same fundamental concern and respect. In the next two chapters we shall see how that legacy is developed.

3

The Social Contract

We have now traced the origins of the basic ideas of contemporary liberalism to their roots in the social contract tradition. We also saw that the social contract tradition is not the only significant source of liberal egalitarian ideas. The liberal connection between equality of concern and respect and material equality is derived from liberal utilitarian thinkers, such as Jeremy Bentham and John Stuart Mill, rather than the contractualists. I have offered only a very abbreviated history of a complex contemporary tradition, yet it is enough to identify the roots of contemporary liberalism. One can always tell more complex histories, especially when dealing with contested political ideas, but that is not the point of this book. Modern liberal egalitarians weave together the complex legacy of these two very different sources of liberal ideas – one emphasizing rights, the other emphasizing outcomes – even if they often present the debate between them as if all the merits are on one side of the argument alone. The key issue in the debate amongst contemporary political theorists, and amongst politicians, is which side should have priority – rights and procedural protections, or outcomes. In this chapter I will argue that contemporary liberal egalitarians come down on the priority of procedures rather than welfare, and show the main outlines of procedural justice.

Although the arguments I am going to present in this chapter for the priority of rights and procedural protections draw on works of abstract political philosophy and theory, it is a serious mistake to see these arguments as arcane, academic and irrelevant to the real world of politics. So I make no apology for spending much of this chapter on Rawls and his liberal critics. Politics is not simply about party competition; it is also about legitimacy and the division and accountability of power. If we abandon serious thought about the conditions of legitimacy and the fairness of our decision-making procedures, we may be faced with a world in which we have nothing to say when political and economic power is concentrated in the hands of a few who face no constraints on how they wield it. Of course, the exercise of political power can be legitimized in a variety of ways, and moral legitimacy may not be the only relevant issue.[1] That said, what makes liberals distinctive is that they attach priority to the moral or normative legitimacy of political systems. Legitimacy takes the form of providing reasons for the exercise of coercive political power that should in principle be acceptable to all that are subject to it. Normative legitimacy is not provided by addressing reasons to a particular group or class, but rather to all who are equally subject to political power. In this way liberals recognize the claims of all to equal concern and respect, especially with regard to the burdens of justification. Contrary to what some like to claim, this does not mean that everyone must actually accept the burdens of public justification – some groups and individuals will want to defend their privileges or positional advantage. Yet the burdens of public justification must be such that no one could reject them as unreasonable. And whatever else reasonableness involves, it denies that some should unilaterally sacrifice their basic rights and interests merely to improve the welfare of others.

This chapter will explore the basic structure of contemporary liberal arguments, through an analysis of the role of the social contract device that has been popularized by John Rawls' *A Theory of Justice*. It will examine the ways in which contemporary liberal theorists conceive of a legitimate and just state, and the strategies they use to justify the principles that underpin a liberal political society. The first section will begin with an analysis of the ways in which the contract device is deployed and understood by liberal theorists as a metaphor for political association and a strategy of justification. The second section will then turn to an analysis of the idea of impartiality as the core value that underpins liberal contractualism. In particular, this section will explore the distinction between first and second impartiality, and how this distinction underpins the idea of a just and liberal political order as a fair procedure for both the public justification of coercive power and for the pursuit of individuals' goals and aspirations. This section will explore the ways in which liberal contractualism is deployed as a political theory that is compatible with a wide variety of views about the demands of morality and the good life, and not as a first-order principle for personal moral deliberation.

Political society as a social contract

The liberal idea of justifying the terms of political association and the exercise of coercive power to all who are subject to it, on terms that acknowledge equality of concern and respect, closely models ideas central to the social contract tradition. It is thus no accident that the most powerful restatement of contemporary liberalism is the contractualist theory of the late John Rawls. Rawls uses the idea of a social contract to model the set of civil rights, constitutional protections and entitlements to economic resources that underpin a just political order. Drawing a connection between justice and fairness, he sets out the terms under which a political regime can be said to acquire normative or moral legitimacy. This connection between the legitimacy of a political association and the idea of justice succeeded in making debates about egalitarian justice central to contemporary political theory, so much so, in fact, that the term liberal political theory has been adopted as a shorthand for theorizing about justice ever since. The contractualist turn in Rawls' theory is captured in the opening section of *A Theory of Justice*, where he writes:

> Justice is the first virtue of social institutions, as truth is of systems of thought. A theory however elegant and economical must be rejected or revised if it is untrue; likewise laws and institutions no matter how efficient and well-arranged

must be reformed or abolished if they are unjust. Each person possesses inviolability founded on justice that even the welfare of society as a whole cannot override. For this reason justice denies that the loss of freedom for some is made right by a greater good shared by others. It does not allow that the sacrifices imposed on a few are outweighed by the larger sum of advantages enjoyed by the many. Therefore in a just society the liberties of equal citizenship are taken as settled; the rights secured by justice are not subject to political bargaining or to the calculus of social interests.[2]

In this passage it is clear that Rawls' concern, and hence that of subsequent liberals, is the normative legitimacy of the basic structure of political society. By the basic structure, Rawls means the distribution of decision-making power, the set of rights and obligations owed to, and by, individuals, and the institutions that distribute them. The basic structure includes the main political institutions, the market economy and the norms or laws, regulating private institutions in civil society. As a normative theory, it has little to say about the origins of political associations, or their historical self-understanding. The focus on the basic structure shows a marked debt on behalf of Rawls to a non-liberal tradition of political thought, namely socialism. The idea that the social structure is of primary concern is arguably at the heart of Marx's critique of capitalism. Yet Rawls combines this concern about the structural conditions of injustice with a liberal focus on the normative significance of the person. Without that normative commitment it is difficult, as we see in the case of Marx, to mount a critique of what is wrong with any structural distribution of power and advantage. In providing this normative legitimacy Rawls turns our attention from the priority of welfare, associated with the utilitarian tradition, back to the ideas we saw developing in the social contract tradition. He does this in two important ways. First, he uses the metaphor of the contract to characterize political society as a fair system of social cooperation. Second, the idea of a contract or hypothetical agreement is used within the theory to generate the principles of justice that give content to the idea of fairness between the members as they pursue their interests and goals.

Thus the idea of a contract is both a theoretical tool and a metaphor. It is a metaphor at the most fundamental level, because it does not presuppose that real political associations are voluntary agreements between people who are free and equal. The social contract is not a crude history of the origin of states. An agreement is clearly not how states came into being. Most states are the result of force, fraud or at best the vicissitudes of history. Yet for liberals this historical record, no matter how honourable, is never sufficient to legitimize the terms of political association or the exercise of coercive power. Instead we can use the metaphor of a contract to model what a legitimate political association should be. To this end, we can understand the idea of a legitimate political association as a fair system of social cooperation amongst people who disagree about fundamental ends, or the purpose of political association. This latter point is most important because it is supposed to characterize the actual experience of modern democratic societies – what is sometimes called the fact of reasonable pluralism. In such societies (that is societies like our own) people disagree about how best to live their lives and how far the collective coercive power of the state should be used to impose moral norms or goals. In societies that are genuinely homogeneous (and there are few, if any), where the facts of reasonable pluralism do not hold, the contract metaphor would not be the most appropriate way of modelling the core liberal values of equality of concern and respect. In such circumstances it is the contract metaphor that has limited scope and not the values it models. That said, liberals believe that the facts of reasonable pluralism hold in the majority of states, especially those that aspire to the status of democracy, and not just western European states. This disagreement about fundamental ends and moral laws is not merely a sociological fact, but is, to all intents and purposes, ineradicable because of the limitations of reason. It is not simply that we are not clever enough to come to some final settlement on the ultimate questions about truth, justice and the meaning of life (or its absence). Rather, the issue is that it is not clear – because of the complex interconnectedness of our beliefs and the possibility of drawing more than one lesson from 'the facts' – what a final justification of such big questions would look like.

The contract metaphor of political association (the state), as a scheme of social cooperation between individuals who disagree about ultimate ends, builds on the idea of reasonable agreement between equals as a necessary condition of legitimacy. The contractarian emphasis on the artificial nature of political society, as a procedure for arbitrating between the rival claims of individuals, has proved to be a powerful image that is shared by many liberals even if they differ significantly from Rawls on the details of his theory of justice. One highly influential liberal philosopher (featuring more prominently in chapter 5), who rejects the contract metaphor, is Ronald Dworkin. He writes that: 'hypothetical contracts do not supply an independent argument for the fairness of enforcing their terms. A hypothetical contract is not simply a pale form of an actual contract: it is no contract at all.'[3] His critique is addressed primarily at the use of the contract device as a justificatory tool within Rawls' argument, but Dworkin does generalize this observation into a rejection of the insights offered by the contract metaphor as an image for a liberal polity. Yet, if we focus on that image, then we can see that despite his protestations Dworkin also deploys a vision of political society as a scheme of cooperation between individuals, who enjoy equality of status and who regulate their affairs in a way that all can reasonably endorse whatever specific goals and projects they may have.[4] Whether Dworkin is best described as a contractualist is not the point; what is important is that the real legacy of the contractualist tradition in liberal theory is the idea of a political community as a fair procedure that depends on the reasonable endorsement of its members. This model of political society is much more widespread than the endorsement of the idea of a hypothetical contract as an explanatory tool, and one can misunderstand the significance of the contractualist turn prompted by Rawls, by focusing narrowly on the structure of decision-making behind the veil of ignorance.

One should remember that the contract is an image or metaphor for helping us understand what a just political order would look like. It is not a thesis about how the state emerges, and clearly it is not the case that modern states are voluntary and artificial in the sense that we collectively agree to create them. What the liberal contract metaphor does emphasize is the limits of sociological and historical factors in determining the nature of justice and legitimacy. These factors are important but not sufficient to guarantee justice. We can always challenge the desirability and legitimacy of how we do things around here. The contract metaphor enables us to do that without becoming utopian, because it acknowledges the limits as well as the benefits of agreement.

Liberalism, neutrality and impartiality

The contract model of political association is an attractive way for liberals to conceive of political association, because it does not presuppose that political society is directed towards any substantive end or goal.[5] Instead political society provides a framework within which the multifarious cooperative ventures of individuals can be pursued. Because the liberal state does not take a substantive view on what constitutes living well, but rather only a procedural view on how people interact within the terms of their rights and liberties, it is often described as being neutral about ultimate ends. The neutral state does not presuppose any basic values or conceptions of the good. In this way the state should be indifferent as to whether some of its citizens are Roman Catholics, Marxists or atheists, as long as they treat others with equal respect. This means that whether someone disagrees with you on how to lead your life has no bearing on your enjoyment of rights and entitlements.

The concept of neutrality is a complex notion that confusingly includes what might be called neutrality of policy outcomes and neutrality of justification for those policy outcomes.[6] In the first case the idea is that the consequences of policy should not privilege any conception of the good or conception of ultimate values. This conception, which has been attributed to some liberals, is incoherent. If we take a contested area of public policy such as the regulation or prohibition of abortion it is clear that no neutral policy position can be arrived at. Either the state prohibits abortion, thus privileging those who believe in the priority of the rights of the unborn, or it permits abortion, thus privileging the rights of mothers to decide whether to carry a pregnancy to term. A policy of indifference would necessarily privilege one side or the other, as there is no third way. Similarly, a liberal policy of toleration has the effect of privileging the views of tolerant liberals over intolerant non-liberals. Talk of neutrality in this sense is a distraction and not a necessary part of liberalism. For this reason, liberal egalitarians are more concerned with neutrality in justification. By this they mean that the justification of liberal principles must emerge from a procedure that does not simply presuppose the truth of a particular conception of the good life. It is no great achievement to show that liberal principles follow from liberal values, although liberals might still be inclined to disagree about details. The really hard thing is to provide those who are not already liberal egalitarians with reasons to accept a liberal political order. Yet, as we have seen, liberalism does take a view on the core ethical significance of individuals. Surely this means that liberals are not neutral between those moral, political and religious doctrines that offer a more holistic account of the individual in relation to community, nation or Church?[7] Again we see how the language of neutrality can raise problems for liberalism. For this reason liberals sympathetic to the Rawlsian project, such as Brian Barry, have abandoned the concept of neutrality in favour of impartiality.[8]

Impartiality theorists do not claim that liberalism is free of any particular fundamental value commitments. Liberalism must give priority to equality of concern and respect and the idea of the separateness of persons – that is, that individuals have ultimate moral significance and cannot be sacrificed for the good of others, individually or collectively. Instead, they attempt to model these basic values in a way that does not presuppose any single conception of the good life, and one that can be accommodated within a wide variety of otherwise non-liberal moral, political and religious viewpoints. It is this attempt to model impartial reasoning that does not presuppose the truth of any particular conception of the good life that brings us to the second and perhaps most famous use of the social contract in Rawls, *A Theory of Justice*.

In order to show why we should accept his two candidate principles for regulating the basic structure of a liberal society, Rawls uses the idea of a contract or agreement behind what he calls the 'veil of ignorance'. The idea is that the principles of justice necessary to guarantee a fair basic structure which does not privilege any particular group is that set which would be agreed upon in a special agreement. However, if people are allowed to enter the agreement with full knowledge of their own position in society, as well as beliefs and values, then they will have a tendency to bargain to maximize their own advantage. For this reason, the initial agreement or choice situation takes place behind what Rawls calls the veil of ignorance. The task of the veil of ignorance is to filter out from individual decision-making the biases of self-preference and partiality.

> Among the essential features of this situation is that no one knows his place in society, his class position or social status, nor does any one know his fortune in the distribution of natural assets and abilities, his intelligence, strength and the like. I shall even assume that the parties do not know their conceptions of the good or their special psychological propensities. The principles of justice are chosen behind a veil of ignorance. This ensures that no one is advantaged or disadvantaged in the choice of principles by the outcome of natural chance or the contingency of social circumstances. Since all are similarly situated and no one is able to design principles to favour his particular condition, the principles of justice are the result of a fair agreement of bargain.[9]

Rawls' basic intuition is that fairness or impartiality can be achieved by combining ignorance with self-interest. If we do not know who we are, but we are nevertheless motivated to improve our condition in life, whoever we are, we will choose Rawls' two principles of justice.

This aspect of Rawls' argument has become the focus for much of the subsequent debate in normative political theory. Many philosophers from libertarian and communitarian camps reject the conception of the person behind the veil of ignorance, because it implies the idea that we are pre-socially individuated.[10] What this means is that Rawls seems to follow the social contract theories of Hobbes or Locke in assuming that the person exists with interests, desires and aspirations before the existence of society. Yet psychologists, anthropologists, historians, and most philosophers since Locke, tell us that this is an implausible notion of human personality as we are inherently social beings.[11] Communitarians such as Michael Sandel combine this challenge to the social ontology of contractualist liberalism with a claim that Rawls' conception of choice behind the veil of ignorance can only work because he has already presupposed the idea that the moral perspective is that of impartiality. Yet without a pre-existing justification of impartiality as the moral point of view, the moral agents in Rawls' theory have no other motive to adopt the perspective of the original position and contract behind the veil of ignorance. The privileging of impartiality rules out moral perspectives such as Aristotelianism that do not grant the same weight to impartiality in practical deliberation. As such, Rawls' theory is accused of failing to be impartial between conceptions of the good in its justification of the principles of justice. I will return to the liberal response to this criticism in chapter 7.

Sandel is not the only critic of Rawls' theory. Many who are fundamentally in sympathy with his overall liberal project have nevertheless been critical of his account of the original position for failing to adequately defend impartiality and thus for offering hostages to those who are not ultimately in sympathy with liberalism. Contractarian liberals, such as Brian Barry, have claimed that Rawls' original position both fails to provide the kind of justificatory argument that is needed, and misconstrues what is essential about the contractarian position.[12]

Barry claims that Rawls' original position argument is redundant because Rawls himself has to supplement the deliberations behind the veil of ignorance with reasons that are external to the design of the original position, such as the 'strains of commitment' argument. This argument claims that any decision made behind the veil of ignorance also has to be a reason that individuals could comply with once they return from the artificial choice situation. Rawls deploys the argument to preclude the possibility of contractors choosing a utilitarian distributive principle. Such a principle might seem attractive given the constraints of the original position but would be unduly burdensome, once the contractors found themselves outside the veil of ignorance, as it would involve them having to accept a potential unilateral sacrifice of their welfare in order to benefit another. This, Rawls acknowledges, would be an unreasonable thing to require as compliance with the choices behind the veil of ignorance would potentially collapse. Given this fact, Rawls uses the strains of commitment as an independent constraint on what could be chosen behind the veil of ignorance. But Barry's point is that this merely shows that the argument from the original position is a diversion that potentially undermines the whole edifice of the two principles of justice. Rather than supporting the substantive theory of justice, this contractarian device renders it more precarious because the veil of ignorance denies individuals a relevant source of information in deciding what candidate principles count as just principles. Rawls' strategy is in danger of appearing as a weak device designed to shore up the two principles, rather than an independent method of justification. Instead Barry argues that we should see Rawls' and the contractualists' justificatory arguments in the light of T. M. Scanlon's idea of reasonable rejectability. Scanlon argues that 'An act is wrong if its performance under the circumstances would be disallowed by any system of rules for the general regulation of behaviour which no one could reasonably reject as a basis for informed, unforced general agreement.'[13] Barry argues that this contractualist account of moral wrongness is a more fruitful justificatory model than Rawls' theory of the original position. He claims that it can incorporate the basic components of Rawls' theory without its unnecessary complexities. These are that reasons must be given for treating people differently – the premise of fundamental equality; that such reasons must be acceptable to those who get the least in any distribution of rights, liberties or the benefits of social cooperation; and it incorporates the idea of preserving the 'separateness of persons' on the grounds that a worsening of one's position cannot be simply justified on the basis of an improvement in another's position. Barry's 'Scanlonian' variant of the social contract places no real weight on the idea of a contract or bargain at all in the process of justification. Instead, Barry claims the metaphor of the contract is useful because it models the idea of a form of impartial deliberation. Barry's argument draws together the intimate link between equality, impartiality and fairness and it is in this way, and this way alone, that he sees himself and also contemporaries such as Rawls as in the contractarian tradition. It is the social contract as a metaphor for a society based on the core values of liberal egalitarianism, rather than the use of the contract as a justificatory strategy, that sustains the appeal of the contract tradition despite the apparent failure of Rawls' original position.[14]

There is one further significant respect in which Barry's impartialist theory echoes the social contract tradition. In the last chapter I argued that contractarian practical deliberation applies a constitutionalist idea of fair agreement to the idea of moral justification. A constitutional or political approach to deliberation can be seen in the accounts of practical reasoning employed by Locke[15] and Kant, and especially in Kant's account of reasonable consent. The modern contractarian approach of Rawls and Barry goes back to the political/constitutional root of the tradition, and in Barry's case we have the most explicit defence of the contract approach as a peculiarly political theory concerned with the rules that shape the basic structure of society, rather than rules that individuals apply in their own practical deliberation.

This emphasis on the political character of liberal egalitarianism is illustrated by Barry's claim that his theory of justice as impartiality applies only at a second-order level. What this means is that the contractarian approach is applicable at the level of structuring the rules that determine the distribution and limits of decision-making power, and not with the making of substantive political and moral decisions. We might distinguish between the two levels in the following way. The first-order rules of a constitution are those which prescribe or proscribe particular actions, for example, that we should not park on double-yellow lines. The second-order rules are the higher rules of the constitution, which distribute the rights and decision-making power that circumscribes first-order legislation. An example would be the rights which underlie habeas corpus, or the fact that not even the state may deprive an individual of her rights without due process of law. The idea of impartiality is appropriate in determining the basic rules or constitutional essentials of a society that is characterized by reasonable pluralism about ultimate ends. Barry is clear that this idea of 'constitutional essentials' also covers the material conditions of fair equality of opportunity and not simply political and civil rights, but we shall treat that issue separately in chapter 5. Of equal importance is the claim that this idea of second-order impartiality does not require individual agents to directly employ a 'reasonable rejectability' test when deliberating how to act. In this way, Barry argues that his theory overcomes a whole raft of criticisms of standard impartialist arguments, to the effect that they are too demanding because they leave no scope for special obligations, personal integrity or care of others.[16] Under the second-order conception, the idea of impartiality applies to the system of rules and decision-making powers – the constitution – and not to individual decisions about how to act. Individuals are not expected to adopt the perspective of impartiality in deciding how to apportion their income after fair taxation, or to adopt the impartialist perspective in deciding whether to promote the position of a loved one over the claims of charity. As we shall see, this is one reason why liberal egalitarians are not simple egalitarians when it comes to moral motivation or the distribution of resources. The expectation that individual agents would adopt the perspective of impartiality in all cases of practical reasoning would indeed be unduly burdensome and thus pose a motivation problem for impartiality theorists. If the theory is unduly demanding then agents are more likely to have other potential motives, which will conflict with and potentially override the impartialist perspective, and not all of these motives will necessarily be non-moral.

The claim that liberal contractualism presupposes first-order impartialism is part of Sandel's critique of Rawls' original position theory, when he argues that Rawls presupposes that the impartialist perspective is *the* perspective of morality. Barry's argument overcomes this challenge, because although he proposes that the impartialist perspective has priority over other perspectives, he does not claim that it is the whole of morality or of politics, and therefore his theory can countenance a variety of viewpoints that attach value to partiality and personal integrity. Agents are not expected to adopt the impartial perspective at all when it comes to real-world practical deliberation. All that individual agents are supposed to accept is that the perspective of impartiality is one from which we justify the 'constitutional essentials' of a polity and its distribution of decision-making and legislative power.

The second-order impartialist perspective also mirrors the idea of constitutionalism, because it does not claim to provide right answers for contested political and moral questions. The impartialist justification applies to the basic structure and the constitutional essentials of a political association. These will, as we have seen, result in a distribution of decision-making power and constitutional protections such as civil and political rights, but they will not prescribe as morally binding, concrete issues of public policy. Many issues of public policy will remain deeply contested among different groups and factions and this must be the case in circumstances of reasonable disagreement. Some of these issues concerning basic rights and interests will be settled by impartial procedures, but these will still leave open legitimate questions for different individuals about how they should exercise their rights. Under a liberal constitution some individuals will have a right (in the form of a permission) to do things which other individuals might regard as morally wrong or unacceptable. The conferral of a right in such cases does not make the action itself a moral or immoral action; rather, it concerns the distribution of discretionary authority from the state or community to the individual. At a fundamental level individuals have basic civil and political rights that place limits on the scope of legislation and public policy. Thus, even a majority decision of a legislature cannot deny basic rights to homosexuals, or deny the vote to women, or racial minorities. These basic civil and political protections follow from the idea of equality of concern and respect. However, not all contested issues can be dealt with by appeal to basic rights and it is this view that distinguishes liberalism from the rights-based libertarianisms of Robert Nozick and Hillel Steiner.[17] Nozick and Steiner argue that individuals and their rights exhaust the moral terrain, so that if an individual has a right that answers the moral question. A similar view is suggested by the role of rights in Ronald Dworkin's earlier writings. Although not a libertarian, Dworkin is sometimes thought to use his concept of 'rights as trump' as a way of settling all the relevant moral questions.[18] To rely on an appeal to basic rights to settle all deeply contested issues is to place unreasonable weight on the idea of consensus. While liberals claim that agreement is possible on certain basic rights and interests, to move from this to the claim that these rights can be extended to solve all deeply contested public moral issues denies the real force of liberalism's recognition of the fact of reasonable pluralism. It is for that reason that liberalism provides procedural solutions to these contested moral issues. The merit of these solutions is that they are procedural and not substantive – they do not claim final moral truth; instead they merely claim the allegiance of all parties, to the extent that the outcome of a decision follows from a fair and impartial procedure that embodies other less contestable moral claims. We might illustrate this procedural perspective with the way in which the issue of abortion has been dealt with in the United Kingdom as opposed to the United States. In the US the famous decision of *Roe* v. *Wade* established a constitutional right to abortion. Many have argued that far from settling the debate this decision has merely entrenched disagreement between the rival parties and unnecessarily politicized the United States' Supreme Court. In the United Kingdom there is a right to abortion, in so far as abortion was legalized in 1967. However, the decision in this case was explicitly a legislative decision. The right is a legal right conferred by a legislative decision, consequently it does not imply a moral or natural right, although clearly those involved in the legislative process might well believe that there is such a moral claim which should be recognized as a legal right. As such, different groups can lobby in different ways and individual legislators can consult their consciences. While the outcome is precarious and could be overridden by a contrary majority, it does have the important outcome of not prejudging the moral perspectives of either party. Pro-life advocates can still claim it is a morally wrong decision; what they cannot claim is that it is an illegitimate decision unless they wish to challenge the whole procedural structure from which the decision emerged. The pro-choice party is in a symmetrical position, and cannot claim that the permissive law settles the fundamental moral question. In this way procedures channel disagreement into decisions where they are necessary, rather than providing final moral answers to questions on which legitimate reasonable disagreement is possible. In this way the defence of second-order impartiality does not contradict the idea of the fact of pluralism about ultimate ends. It merely acknowledges the impartial constitution as an alternative to the potential conflict that would arise from imposing uniformity of belief, judgement and values in circumstances of pluralism.

The contractualist model of political society, and the important distinction between first- and second-order impartiality, illustrate the way in which contemporary liberal egalitarians offer a political conception of social justice. By this they mean a moral theory that applies to the basic structures of a political community. What Rawls, Barry and other contractarian liberals do not mean is a full moral theory of personal action. Unlike first-order impartialist moral and ethical theories, such as act-utilitarianism or Kant's categorical imperative, the political conception of second-order impartiality is not concerned with norms that should guide individuals in their own practical deliberation. Clearly, the distribution of decision-making power and personal rights and liberties that follows from the liberal contractualist method of justification has a bearing on how each individual should treat his or her neighbour. Liberalism does offer a set of moral norms, and it is not wholly neutral on the issue of ethics: indeed it could not be, given that it is premised on the ethical significance of each person. What is important about the liberal vision is that this ethical view is limited to the political domain and not the personal domain or the idea of a full conception of the good life. Fundamental disagreement about the good life, or reasonable pluralism, poses both practical and normative constraints on the idea of a full comprehensive conception of the good being imposed on a plural democratic society. Liberalism's aspiration to provide a political conception of social justice is not a second-best option in the face of disagreement, but a positive response to the demands of modern democratic societies. In the final analysis, the success of the liberal project turns on the ability of a liberal theory to fit with our considered expectations of the character of modern democratic states. The contract metaphor provides us with a way of understanding how modern democratic states can be seen to nurture and protect the equal status and claims of all individuals as equal citizens.

4
Liberalism and Liberty

The contractualist turn in contemporary political theory, associated with the prominent liberal theories of Rawls and Barry, addresses the fact of reasonable pluralism in modern democratic states. People have different views about the ultimate direction or point of civil life or political association. A perfectionist approach to both constitutional essentials and public policy will offend against the considered opinions and values of large groups in society, and therefore, in the long run, make social and political arrangements less stable. By perfectionist view, I mean a social and political morality that makes demands on the whole range of another person's life, in terms of the ends she can pursue and the beliefs and values she should hold. Political liberalism does not rule out all forms of state paternalism in the way that libertarianism does. The requirement to label poisons, dangerous drugs, and require that domestic electrical appliances be earthed does not constitute the kind of paternalism that sensible liberals object to. Instead, liberals are concerned with the coercive imposition of moral, political and cultural commitments that do not afford full equality of concern and respect to each person. Contractualism provides a model of a liberal society that accommodates the facts of reasonable pluralism about ultimate ends. It does, however, remain a procedural ideal both in terms of how it accommodates the claims of individuals to be treated as equals, and in terms of how it justifies the principles that regulate the actions of individuals in a fair and just manner. The last chapter outlined this model of political association or the state as a fair system of social cooperation. In this chapter I will turn to the liberal account of the principles which shape that vision of political society as a fair system of social cooperation. Taken together, chapters 3, 4 and 5 cover the main strands of contemporary liberal political theory. The last chapter addressed what are often called 'foundational issues', that is, questions about how one explains and justifies a liberal political order. This chapter and the next will turn to substantive issues, namely an account of the principles that shape a liberal political order and that are supposed to emerge from the strategies of liberal justification.

This chapter and the next (which addresses economic equality) will loosely correspond to the order Rawls attaches to his two principles of justice, although they will range more widely than a simple account of what Rawls said, but they do not entail an endorsement of Rawls' account of priority. This chapter will deal with the issue of liberty and its status within liberalism. The next chapter will deal with the issue of equality of resources, or the economic components of liberal egalitarianism.

Types of freedom

In the introduction to this book I claimed that the core value underpinning the form of political liberalism that is dominant in modern western democracies, and in political theory, is equality rather than liberty. It is for this reason that we traced the roots of liberalism in the contractualist tradition and in utilitarianism, but it is also for this reason that I have not addressed other sources of the wider ideology of liberalism which place primary importance on liberty as such. Part of the justification for this approach is that this more libertarian understanding of liberalism has in theory and practice been incorporated into the development of modern conservatism.[1] In the US the form of liberalism that I am explaining is seen as a leftist ideology or political theory, whereas US conservatives in both the Republican and Democrat parties place primary value on liberty above all else. A good example of this is provided by the president, George W. Bush jnr, who is described as a conservative (by his supporters), but whose political rhetoric is almost exclusively about freedom and its extension. Most conservatives in the United States and Europe would claim that liberty is their primary concern, as we can see from the example of the British Conservative Party and its leadership.

Libertarians of both left and right (which includes most modern variants of conservatism) see liberty as the basic political value. The concept of liberty can be understood in a variety of ways. The three most common contemporary views are negative, positive and republican liberty.[2] I will begin this chapter with an account of these three conceptions of liberty, as they shape much of the discussion.

Of these rival interpretations, the idea of negative liberty is that most closely associated with liberalism, and both right-wing and left-wing libertarianism.[3] Its most famous advocate is Isaiah Berlin. Negative liberty is the idea of freedom as the absence of coercion in terms of both restraints and constraints. An individual is restrained when she is subject to the direct prevention of action by imprisonment, manacles, locks and barred windows. If one is locked in gaol then one is unfree in the relevant sense, however one feels about that imprisonment. Constraint on the other hand is not the prevention of action, but its compulsion. If a person is forced to act in a certain way then that person is also not free. Both restrictions and compulsion form types of coercion and wherever there is coercion there is an absence of freedom. Coercion is a notoriously difficult concept to define and many negative libertarians tend towards the view that only direct restrictions count as cases of unfreedom. The sixteenth-century philosopher Thomas Hobbes is an exemplar of this view, in that he argues that one can be free 'at the point of a sword' as the mere threat of interference does not prevent one choosing an unpalatable outcome.[4] Negative liberty theorists differ in terms of the accounts they give of the narrowness or expansiveness of what can count as coercion. These differences can be traced back to issues about the metaphysics of the person and the free-will–determinacy debate in the philosophy of action.

These are important issues but they need not detain us here, as most negative liberty theorists do not take a common view on them. What is important is that negative liberty theorists see all the relevant restrictions on liberty as being external to the person. A person is not rendered unfree by their own beliefs or moral status: for a negative liberty theorist, one cannot be unfree simply because one finds some decisions unpalatable or because some options are contrary to one's fundamental beliefs. Thus, choosing to do things that are bad or by other standards immoral is not a case of acting unfreely. This view has the important consequence that in its negative guise liberty is restricted by both law and by the pursuit of the common good, such as social welfare or equality. Even though law may give more value to liberty, by restricting the opportunity for others to do one harm, or by distributing resources that make some choices easier to make, it nevertheless restricts freedom. For strict libertarians, such as Robert Nozick, if liberty is restricted by measures of social justice and equality then these later values must give way to liberty because they involve coercion. Nozick famously claims that taxation for purposes of distributive justice, and anything else short of the maintenance of the most limited protective state, is actually a form of forced labour.[5]

Other liberals who employ the concept of negative liberty, such as Isaiah Berlin, do not deny that liberty should sometimes give way to other values such as security, equality or social justice – as a value pluralist Berlin is committed to the importance of values other than liberty. What Berlin does insist is that where such restrictions on freedom are necessary we need to be clear that we are sacrificing liberty to some other good, and not advancing a different conception of liberty. Negative liberty theorists such as Berlin explicitly deny the Rousseauean claim that one can be forced to be free – that way leads to totalitarianism not freedom. Freedom is not the achievement of a certain sort of self-rule or autonomy, in accordance with the moral law, as positive liberty theorists such as Rousseau and Kant have argued. Negative liberty has a certain attractive simplicity about it. To paraphrase Bishop Butler, liberty 'is what it is, and not another thing'.[6] It is not social justice, or morality, or equality, or human flourishing; it is simply the absence of the relevant kinds of interference. This simplicity has no doubt made the concept attractive to libertarians and conservatives who want to challenge the dominance of the modern state.

Much of what states do is coercive in the relevant sense of restricting action through law or constraining actions through compulsory education, health and safety, and, in many cases, even such things as military service and voting. States restrict freedom. Yet one should remember that there is nothing that necessarily requires those who endorse a negative analysis of liberty also to endorse a conservative or anti-state political agenda. One could accept the negative libertarian analysis and yet argue for other reasons that some goods always justify the restriction of *some* liberty: take, for example, goods such as security or equality. As Berlin points out, all that the negative analysis commits us to is the idea that liberty is not the same as other discrete values such as justice, equality or security. The argument that liberty must trump all other values, as libertarians and conservatives suggest, requires a different argument than the mere conceptual analysis of liberty. It is important to bear this point in mind as we explore the way that political liberals use the concept of liberty. Accepting the negative analysis of the concept of liberty does not necessarily commit one to a particular ideological agenda.

In contrast to the negative concept of liberty, positive liberty does not focus on the idea of external coercion in terms of prevention and compulsion. It places much more emphasis on the idea of acting in accordance with the moral law. The positive idea of freedom as self-rule draws on controversial classical and Christian ideas about self-mastery, and associated ideas of acting in accordance with objective norms of rationality, morality and the common good. In this sense, being free is just as much about being in control of one's passions or base desires as about being free from external constraints. For those influenced by Christian moral teaching, true freedom consists in the ordering of our souls away from our more sinful natures. But this idea is not only Christian. Ancient conceptions of freedom, such as those offered by Plato or Aristotle, also view the idea of true freedom as overcoming nature and ordering our souls, psyches or real selves, in accordance with reason or morality. To that extent freedom is not inimical to law but actually requires it, contrary to the views of negative liberty theorists. Although the positive idea has ancient origins, it finds its most forceful restatement in the modern period in the ideas of the eighteenth-century French thinker Jean-Jacques Rousseau (1712–1778). For Rousseau, being free in the sense of being self-governing is perfectly compatible with being subject to the coercive will of others, as long as that will is your real or true will manifested in the General Will (in which case it does not count as coercion).[7] This idea of the General Will, manifested politically as our true will, is the source of Rousseau's paradoxical views about the idea of coercing people into real freedom. If acting in accordance with the law is being truly free, then coercion by the state and the police is not merely a condition of peace and order but is a condition of one actually being free. When the state makes one act in a certain way, it actually makes one free. In making this argument, Rousseau has a very specific conception of the state in mind and he is drawing on ideas that are familiar in Christian theology. That said, in light of the history of the twentieth century, the idea that coercion by the state is the source of freedom has repelled most liberals. Rousseau's doctrine of positive liberty is often considered a precursor of the modern totalitarianism of Hitler and Stalin.[8] It is no doubt for this reason that, while Berlin offers his two-concepts thesis as an analysis and history of modern liberty, he clearly endorses the negative conception above positive liberty. Whether positive liberty doctrines tend towards totalitarianism, as J. L Talmon and Karl Popper suggest, depends upon the view one takes of the authority that decides when an individual's actions are indeed in accordance with her true or real interests. If this authority is 'the party', then being forced to be free might well have the tendencies claimed. Whether this is so or not, the crucial point that positive liberty theories claim is that the individual agent is not always the final judge of what her interests are, and what actions, rules and obstacles count as restrictions on liberty. Thus one may feel constrained by certain laws while those laws are, at the same time, constitutive of one's liberty. Once again, it is important to bear in mind that positive liberty, for all its apparent tendencies, does not necessarily commit one to any particular ideological agenda. As the Canadian philosopher Charles Taylor has consistently argued, the concept of positive liberty merely indicates the connection between freedom and morality or rationality.[9] What is required by morality and rationality is of course another question. But there is no reason why the positive concept of liberty cannot be deployed by a liberal theory. That said, as it depends upon an account of the self and its real interests, any liberal theory that does deploy a positive conception of liberty is going to be highly perfectionist, and this is likely to prove problematic when confronted by the fact of reasonable pluralism. Consequently, positive conceptions of freedom are more closely associated with communitarianism than with political liberalism.

A third concept of liberty alongside Berlin's account of negative and positive liberty has been offered by a group of theorists influenced by republicanism.[10] Republican theorists such as Skinner, Pettit and Viroli have attempted to recover and defend an alternative conception of political liberty, under which certain forms of citizen action are deemed as conditions of personal freedom, on the grounds that the exercise of political liberty is essential for a regime of personal liberty.[11] This contrasts with the views of negative and positive liberty theorists who reduce all discussions of freedom to that of personal liberty, and with the denial by negative liberty theorists that there is a specific concept of political liberty. The republican theorists' aim is to combine political liberty and civic virtue with a view of freedom as nondomination, in order to avoid what they take to be the potentially anarchistic or anti-political implications of unrestricted negative liberty theories. The potentially anarchistic consequence of negative freedom is famously illustrated by Robert Nozick in *Anarchy, State and Utopia*, a book where be argues that a minimal, or night-watchman state, is the only form of government compatible with strong individual rights to liberty. For republicans, this tendency towards libertarianism has a deleterious effect on public discourse, as it casts all common political endeavour such as taxation and welfare provision as restrictions of liberty. This is a consequence that conservative libertarians in the United States and Europe have been happy to endorse. But more importantly it also rules out the cultivation of the virtues of civic engagement as a means of protecting a regime of liberty. Any common cultivation of an active citizenry, concerned to preserve and defend their constitutional and personal liberty from 'over-mighty subjects', such as 'media barons', would still count as an infringement of negative liberty. The discourse of negative liberty commits one to a race to the bottom, in terms of thinning out our civic culture in a way that actually threatens our personal liberties far more than some forms of constitutional restrictions and distributions of power.

The most philosophically sophisticated statement of a republican conception of freedom, which is not merely the recovery of a historical tradition or an endorsement of a peculiar brand of communitarian politics, is provided by Philip Pettit in his book *Republicanism*. His 'third' concept of freedom (after Berlin's famous argument that there are only two concepts, negative and positive) claims that freedom is not merely the absence of interference with the exercise of our will, but rather the absence of domination. Part of his reason for adopting this view is the familiar republican claim that negative liberty theories see all interference, even when designed to maintain a regime of liberty, as restrictions on freedom. Republicans are not merely concerned with interference, but with who interferes and how: hence the priority they attach to political liberty.

To enjoy a relationship of domination over another is to be in a position to affect her interests independently of her will, choice or endorsement. Classically, this is the position of the slave, who may enjoy considerable personal discretion in her actions and may enjoy a benign master, but who nevertheless remains subject to the will of another. For the republican, the non-interference model can only give an inadequate account of the wrongness of slavery, as its account must depend on coercive intervention. While most slaves have been subject to cruel, coercive and often murderous treatment, this is not always so, as some slaves have enjoyed wide discretion and humane masters. The point is that their status is always subject to the contingencies of the master's will. For republicans it is the relationship and not the consequences that matter.

But does this concern mark a significant advance beyond the non-interference view? Many negative liberty theorists have included the risk of interference as a source of unfreedom (unlike Hobbes, Bentham speaks of restraints and constraints as restrictions on freedom). For Pettit, where the republican differs from the liberal is that the former is concerned with 'resilient' non-interference.[12] Resilient non-interference is not merely 'staying the hand' of a sovereign power that could interfere, but the absence of interference on the basis of institutional constraints. What makes non-interference 'resilient' is the presence of institutional constraints that preclude the exercise of interference. It is crucial to note that it is not merely the absence of interference that is relevant, but why there is no interference. After all non-interference could merely be a result of self-censorship in the face of the threat of interference. Pettit places great emphasis on the absence of self-censorship in the face of political power, and uses this to draw the connection between freedom as the absence of dominating power relationships and the republican tradition's concern with corruption. In the face of a threat of interference subjects can merely assume the interest of the dominator and therefore censor their own behaviour. It is a common argument of feminists that patriarchy can implicate women in their own oppression in precisely this way. Furthermore, the presence of a disposition to self-censor is likely to reduce the risk of interference, because it reduces the need to interfere.

The crucial concern for Pettit is self-censorship. In a free state the number of cases of non-interference may not be significantly greater, but the absence of interference will no longer be a function of self-censorship. But is absence of self-censorship sufficient to carry Pettit's argument? For dominating power is unlikely to cause self-censorship without at least the significant risk or threat of interference. Self-censorship therefore tracks the idea of coercive interference. In the absence of interference or its threat, we have no need to self-censor. Of course, Pettit may be right to suggest that self-censorship is the cause of non-interference, but we still need the harm of interference to make the case that this constitutes a case of unfreedom. For the historical republican theorists, the issue of self-censorship only arises in the face of actual and potential risks of interference – living under the rule of the 'Turk', the 'Pope' or the 'Emperor'.

The theory of freedom offered by Pettit separates the issue between non-domination and non-interference theories from judgements concerning the probabilities of interference. The plausibility of the non-domination account depends upon the presence of risk and judgements of probability of interference. Alongside the question of whether resilient non-interference is a modally different conception of freedom from that offered by standard non-interference theories, an equally important question for Pettit is how one delimits the category of domination. Domination is a structural relation of unequal power and authority. Yet domination as such cannot be the relevant category, because the law imposes an unequal power relation on those subject to it. Similarly, I can put myself under such power relations that are wholly benign – for example, I can submit myself to the authority of a piano teacher. Pettit qualifies his concern by arguing that the republican theorists are concerned with arbitrary domination, rather than domination as such. In order to fix the class of arbitrary domination, Pettit argues that an exercise of coercive power is non-dominating when it tracks the common recognizable interests of those citizens over whom it is exercised.[13] Clearly, Pettit does not have in mind some Rousseauean distinction between perceived and real interests as this would lead back to positive liberty. Like the negative theory of liberty, Pettit's non-domination model identifies a large class of potential instances of domination, but falls back on a liberal, social or political theory to distinguish the relevant classes of interference that do not constitute limitations on freedom. But if Pettit's theory broadly mirrors the substantive positions of Rawls and the utilitarians, one might well ask what precisely we gain by characterizing freedom as non-domination? What improvement does the republican rhetoric of freedom as non-domination offer over and above that already available to liberals using the language of non-interference and security against misrule?

One reason to be sceptical of its benefits as an alternative discourse of freedom is that it masks the essential trade-offs one has to make between personal and political liberty. The advantage of non-interference theories is that these trade-offs remain transparent. Pettit's account has the tendency to mask such trade-offs, indeed denying that they are trade-offs, by interpreting interference that tracks our interests as not a case of unfreedom. Thus actions to secure equality of status and fair treatment by redistributing resources and power are not interference with freedom. More importantly, restrictions on personal liberty for the public good are not restrictions of freedom.

If the republican discourse provided conceptual distinctions and uncovered categories of interference that the liberal discourse of freedom as non-interference could not identify, there might be a good case for endorsing a third concept of liberty. But as we can already do what the republicans want within liberal theories, and, as the issue of non-domination remains only a species of the negative non-interference theory, we gain little by adopting it and lose much that remains important.

I have devoted most attention to the discussion of the republican conception of freedom for two important reasons. The first is the recent attempt by republicans to overcome liberalism by reverting to an older political tradition of liberty, of which liberalism is only a subset.[14] However, what republicanism ignores is precisely why liberalism emerges within the republican tradition. Liberals are concerned to specify a set of constraints around what any liberal constitutional structure can do with its powers. The republican tradition rejects the domination of external powers of empire, but has little to say about the problems of internal dominance without falling back on the discourse of equal rights and liberties that preclude the dominance of factions and majority opinion. Republicanism provides an important social theory of freedom, but one that properly understood tends towards support for the liberal position and an account of freedom as the absence of interference. The second important conclusion from the discussion of the republican concept of freedom is that all three concepts are only partially detachable from complex social and political theories of freedom. Ultimately, it is as a social or political theory of freedom that we should judge liberalism and not in terms of the contours of any particular conceptual analysis.

Liberalism and freedom

Liberalism is best seen as a social and political theory of freedom that conceives of liberty largely in terms of non-interference. But if this is so then it would seem that freedom and equality must come into conflict. Faced with this, one has to make a choice between two incommensurable values. Only utilitarians have the luxury of translating the concepts of freedom and equality into a higher value such as utility, which can then balance the claims of both equality and liberty. Liberal egalitarians do not have that luxury, but nor do they have the luxury of saying that equality always trumps liberty. Liberals consider liberty a central value even if they subordinate it to a conception of equal concern and respect. Thus prominent liberals, such as Rawls, Dworkin, Nagel and Barry, need a way of combining the claims of liberty with their fundamental egalitarianism. But they need to do this in a way that gives liberty a high value if they are to avoid the prospect of moral perfectionism and paternalism – both of which would run up against the political aspiration to accommodate reasonable disagreement about the good life.

In order to avoid the risk of moral perfectionism or paternalism, liberals do not employ a positive conception of liberty as self-rule under the moral law, as this would beg the question of 'whose moral law'? Neither do they employ a republican conception of liberty as civic virtue, although liberals can agree that certain forms of civic virtue are helpful in sustaining a regime of liberty. For liberals such as Rawls and Barry, liberty remains a largely negative concept enjoyed because of the absence of real and threatened interference. A just regime might well involve some of the virtues of active citizenship, but this is best described as something other than liberty. That said, liberals are not simple negative liberty theorists either. Rawls, for example, explicitly adopts G. C. MacCallum's reconciliationist or 'triadic' analysis of freedom, where a person is free when that person is not subject to a restraint or constraint preventing him or her from performing some specified action. Freedom must therefore specify the agent, the restriction the agent is *free from* and the action they are therefore *free to do*.[15] This 'triadic' conception of freedom is supposed to overcome the false opposition that underlies Berlin's thesis about the two concepts of freedom. MacCallum's view of freedom as the absence of interference in doing certain specified kinds of action is illustrated in the idea of basic liberties that have become central to the clarification of Rawls' first principle of justice. These basic liberties specify certain kinds of non-interference that are essential in order to do specific classes of action. MacCallum's analysis opens up the possibility of giving a political or social theory of freedom, specifying which kinds of non-interference are most important and why, and thus avoids the libertarian tendency of negative analyses to characterize all cases of interference as equally wrong. The triadic analysis retains the predominantly negative character of the concept of liberty, but also goes beyond negative liberty in specifying which forms of non-interference are morally and politically important.

We can see the development and implications of this view in Rawls' account of the first principle of justice. At the beginning of *A Theory of Justice* Rawls gave a preliminary statement of the first of his two principles of justice as follows: 'each person is to have an equal right to the most extensive basic liberty compatible with a similar liberty for others'.[16] He went on to clarify and refine this statement, but even so the idea of a right to most extensive liberty, limited only by the similar liberty of others, encountered major criticism on the grounds of its indeterminacy, most famously from the British legal philosopher H. L. A. Hart.[17] The concept of greatest liberty cannot be distinguished from judgements and claims about which liberties are more important than others, and which liberties are more important than others depends upon what ends these liberties serve. Hart gives the example of procedural rules of debate, where a general restriction on speaking whenever one wants is adopted in order to facilitate debate and thus allow all participants to have a say. This is a good example of some freedom being sacrificed to facilitate a more valuable freedom, the freedom to be heard. The point that Hart makes so forcefully is that liberty as the total absence of restraint and constraint is not necessarily a good. The absence of restraints on my ability to harm you is not perceived by me as valuable if I am a bully or a tyrant. Liberty becomes valuable in relation to certain basic human interests. Thus, it is liberties that are valuable and not necessarily liberty as such. Rawls concedes Hart's criticisms in Lecture VIII of *Political Liberalism*, 'The Basic Liberties and Their Priority'. Instead of equal basic liberty, he revises the first principle of justice to read 'Each person has an equal right to a fully adequate scheme of equal basic liberties which is compatible with a similar scheme for all.'[18] The revised version of the first principle reflects a conception of freedom that is much closer to that implicit in MacCallum's triadic analysis, where the concept of liberty is reduced to specific liberties to do specific things. But it retains the liberal hostility to perfectionism by giving prominence to the idea of the absence of restrictions and compulsion.

We can thus return to the question of liberalism's reconciliation of freedom and equality. Liberty retains importance in political liberalism in terms of a set of basic liberties. These basic liberties are things that should be enjoyed by everyone equally. Equality of concern and respect therefore involves the equal distribution of a set of basic liberties to each person. These liberties provide both a sphere of personal discretion within which individuals pursue their conceptions of the good, and, importantly, a series of political liberties that serve to secure those spheres. Most liberals do not give a final specification to this set of the basic liberties. But it is important to note that they do combine political liberties with personal liberties, in setting out the overall character of a liberal conception of freedom. People are given a sphere of personal discretion over how to live their lives. They are also afforded liberties against the overbearing nature of state power, in terms of rights to freedom of speech, due process, and freedom to stand for political office or to cast a vote in elections. It is by striking a balance between the claims of personal liberty and political liberty that liberalism is distinguished from republican or democratic theories, both of which give priority to political liberty. Liberals retain much more scepticism than republicans about the collective exercise of political power and therefore make personal liberty an important part of the list of basic liberties. One liberty that political liberals do not include among the basic liberties, which earlier liberal traditions would have regarded as essential, is the idea of freedom to acquire and dispose of private property. We will explore in more detail in the next chapter why Rawls, Barry and other political liberals preclude private property from their list of basic liberties. But the absence of freedom of property is certainly a departure from the ideas of Locke and Kant, as well as most libertarians such as Nozick and Hayek. It also partly explains the enthusiasm of contemporary conservatives for libertarian theorists such as Nozick and Hayek, and their hostility to liberals such as Rawls or Barry.

The idea of a system of equal basic liberties shows how the idea of freedom fits into the contractarian account of liberalism that we have explored in the last chapter. That said, we are still left with some important questions, such as what are the basic liberties; does the account of the basic liberties avoid the charge of indeterminacy; and, finally, why do the basic liberties have priority over the other basic goods that comprise equal treatment?

Indeterminacy and priority

Many critics of contemporary political liberalism argue that the appeal to a set of equal basic liberties is no less indeterminate than Rawls' original reference to a sphere of equal liberty.[19] Any specification of the set of equal basic liberties will be specific to a particular historical and political tradition and reflect the presuppositions of those traditions. The US Bill of Rights will no doubt influence American writers in specifying the basic constitutional and personal liberties. European liberals are more likely to give a different set of basic liberties or to establish different hierarchies amongst them. American liberals would defend an absolute unrestricted right to freedom of speech and expression, where British and European liberals might wish to limit unrestricted freedom of expression in order to include a right to privacy amongst the equal basic liberties. These examples illustrate the problems if not the impossibility of specifying a unique set of liberal equal basic liberties. But is that really a problem? A more pressing version of the indeterminacy criticism is not that we cannot identify a single unique set of liberal basic liberties. Rather, it is the claim that for any set of basic liberties there will be an irreducible indeterminacy within that set. What this means is that liberties such as freedom of speech are just as indeterminate as liberty itself, in that there is no uncontroversial specification that reconciles the claims of free speech with rights to privacy or the avoidance of, for example, hate speech. This raises the issue of the priority of particular liberties. If questions can be raised about the priority of unrestricted free speech over personal privacy, then can we also justify the claim that liberty has priority over economic goods? The fact that not everything can count as a restriction of speech still leaves open a large realm of what can. We can only settle these disputes by appeal to particular accounts of why these liberties are more basic than others. Yet acknowledging this seems to contradict the alleged impartiality of liberal egalitarianism. Instead it must reveal itself as a controversial conception of the good in which a particular conception of the priority of liberty holds. For John Gray, this is precisely what is revealed by the history of particular national liberalisms. Each has its own way of arguing for the limits and priority of particular liberties, but each depends upon a particular set of ethical commitments that are local, historically contingent and definitely not impartial.

There might well be a large variety of sets of basic liberties that we can derive from the constitutional and political histories of modern liberal and democratic states. The issue of no single unique set only matters if political liberalism has to be uniquely identified with one particular set of liberties. But it does not. Instead, liberals such as Rawls and Barry give us candidates for what might count as basic liberties within the context of a process of reasonable justification. In other words, we are given a framework within which we can provide an account of what those basic liberties are. That leaves open the detailed specification of particular liberties, but it does not leave us with total indeterminacy. The content of the set of basic liberties is set by the prior commitment to securing equality of concern and respect of each person. This will entail liberty of speech and conscience, freedom of association and the freedom from arbitrary arrest and detention, and due process.[20] It will also entail a number of political liberties necessary to hold political power to account. It is not the case that anything can count as a basic liberty. All of these liberties are important because they constitute the equality of each person as a moral subject and citizen. Given the irreducibility of disagreement about full comprehensive moral doctrines, the set of basic liberties are defined as those rights, protections and privileges necessary for individuals to form and pursue their own life plans and conceptions of the good, consistently with others being able to do likewise. These liberties must be generically valuable. It is central to the liberal argument that we can provide an account of basic liberties that is not simply reducible to the set offered by any particular political tradition. Rawls grounds his defence of a set of equal basic liberties on his account of the two 'moral' powers that characterize each person as a possible moral agent. These are the capacity for a sense of justice and a capacity for a conception of the good. For Barry and Scanlon the conception of the person is implicit in the agreement motive, that is, the desire to seek terms of social cooperation which no one can reasonably reject. Both approaches provide a basis for why we might identify specific liberties of speech, association and political participation as being central to each person's conception of what is good, whatever the content of that conception. It will, however, rule out fundamentally inegalitarian views that deny certain liberties to specific groups of people. It is this responsibility for the final goals we pursue in life that gives the basic liberties their priority. Individuals can adopt and endorse non-autonomy enhancing lifestyles, but they cannot have those imposed on them politically without being denied equality of concern and respect. That is what gives the basic liberties their priority.

What about the substance of Gray's charge about the indeterminacy of the basic liberties themselves: how much freedom of speech versus how much privacy? Much of the plausibility of this critique depends upon regarding the basic liberties individually. But, as Rawls points out in 'The Basic

Liberties and Their Priority', the basic liberties have to be regarded as a system.[21] It is through the construction of a system that the scope of the basic liberties is specified, as well as the rules for arbitrating between them. What is chosen in a liberal social contract is the set of principles that guide a constitutional structure, and not the specific constitutional and political rights of a municipal legal system. The relevant principle here is the priority and outline of a set of basic liberties that apply to all. It is no more an argument against the possibility of such a system, that individual liberties are indeterminate, than it is an argument against the possibility of legal rights that these are also potentially indeterminate because they come into conflict and require interpretation in adjudication. As long as we see the basic liberties forming part of a system that is not subject to the vagaries of political manipulation, then there is no reason to rule out sufficient determinacy among the basic liberties. Therefore, we can potentially set limits to the scope of these liberties. Even a system such as that of the United States places limits on the scope of freedom of speech and expression. It does not, for example, allow incitement to commit treason.

We can provide a set of equal basic liberties, but it will be a set rather than a single list or single unique constitution. Much of the plausibility of Gray's critique depends upon the claim that liberalism tends towards a single unique constitutional form that is valid in all times and all places. That is not required, and it is not claimed by any of the main theorists of liberalism. What liberalism does aim to provide is a set of principles which serve as guidelines for the candidate liberties, rights and privileges that will distribute liberty in a liberal constitution. The set of genuinely liberal constitutions will have boundaries determining what is acceptable and will be subject to change over time, but that process of change will have a particular direction guided by the regulative norms of justice. It will preclude some of the more unfortunate practices of some so-called liberal democracies that seek to derogate from human rights and basic civil liberties, such as the bar on detention without trial.

By turning its attention away from interference per se as always wrong, the political liberal's concentration on the equal enjoyment and protection of a set of specific basic liberties focuses our attention on the important question about which liberties matter most. In this way we can identify a set of restraints and constraints on political power, whether exercised by the state, private interests, factions or by majority opinion, which are necessary for the protection of the equal status of each individual. This approach combines aspects of the negative concept of freedom as non-interference with the republicans' concern for the political protection of regimes of liberty. Liberals would not be liberals if they did not attach significance to freedom. Yet what makes freedom valuable for political liberals is what also makes it subordinate to the claims of equality of concern and respect.

5
Liberalism and Equality

The concept of freedom is undoubtedly central to any serious contender for the title of liberalism. That is so, whether liberty is a foundational value, or, as contemporary liberals claim, it is derived from a prior value such as utility (in the case of J. S. Mill) or equality, as we saw with the twentieth-century liberals such as John Rawls. The modern liberal turn towards an equal set of basic liberties seems to revert to an older classical liberal tradition that we find in Locke, rather than what Quentin Skinner regards as the more dubiously liberal legacy of Thomas Hobbes or Jeremy Bentham that is central to the idea of negative liberty popularized by Isaiah Berlin.[1] The idea of a set of equal basic liberties does reflect Locke's distinction between the right to liberty as a moral concept and the background absence of restrictions that he dismissively describes as licence.[2] It is only in the twentieth century that liberalism has become synonymous with the idea of negative liberty as such. It was certainly no part of the agenda of classical liberals, from Locke to those of the nineteenth century. But the analogy and connection with Locke should not be stretched too far, for there is a fundamental respect in which contemporary political liberalism abandons the Lockean legacy. Indeed, it is precisely this abandonment of the strictly Lockean legacy that distinguishes egalitarian political liberalism from contemporary libertarianism, such as that associated with Robert Nozick's *Anarchy, State and*

Utopia. For Locke and for his contemporary followers such as Nozick, property is a pre-political natural right and, therefore, something beyond the scope of either state interference or considerations of social justice. While libertarians such as Nozick place the protection and security of property at the centre of politics (indeed, for Nozick, protecting basic rights to life, liberty and property exhaust the scope of politics), liberals do not attach quite the same significance to property. That does not mean that Rawls, Dworkin and Barry wish to dispense with the idea of property rights, but it does mean that these rights are conditional in a way in which the other basic liberties are not. Ownership rights and property holdings are features of the basic structure of society and therefore subject to considerations of distributive justice in a different way from the basic liberties. This is illustrated by Rawls' ordering of the two principles of justice in his theory, where the right to an equal system of basic liberties is described as being 'lexically' prior to the difference principle which distributes resources and sets limits to the scope of private property rights. How much we can own, and what rights we have to economic resources is not a pre-political matter that is none of the state's business. The claims of property do not, for liberals, place constraints on the constitution of the basic structure of society. Instead the claims of property are secondary to claims of fairly distributing economic primary goods across the basic structure. That said, liberals are not indifferent to how wealth, property and access to economic resources are distributed, as many critics of liberal theories of justice suggest. It is not the case that because liberals dispense with the idea of a natural, or pre-political, distribution of property and resources they leave the matter up to the collective determination of politics. To do so would leave the distribution of property to levelling, the fear of traditional nineteenth-century liberals, where the majority threatens to dispossess the holders of capital and thus indirectly impoverish everyone. Contemporary liberals, too, are concerned about the way in which the wealthy and powerful can use their wealth and property to distort the tax system or welfare provision to use economic power for their own sectional advantage. Classical liberals saw the assertion of the right to private property as a means of defending individuals from greedy and rapacious sovereigns or the ignorant masses, neither of whom saw the connection between private wealth, capital accumulation and employment. Contemporary liberals see the need for a just distribution of property and access to resources as a challenge to the tendency of significant material inequality to undermine citizen equality and instead secure factional advantage across the whole of society. Contemporary political liberalism comprises a combination of equal basic liberties and equal access to a basic set of economic resources or economic primary goods.

In the rest of this chapter I will examine the characteristic arguments that liberals have deployed for their liberal egalitarian distribution of resources or economic primary goods. This chapter will also consider why liberals reject more straightforwardly egalitarian views about equality in favour of drawing a distinction between inequalities that are the result of choice, and those which are the result of chance. It will be seen that this distinction is essential for combining the claims of justice with the freedom to frame and pursue meaningful lives. Before turning to a discussion of the two most important liberal theorists of social justice we need to examine a potential challenge to the very coherence of social justice.

The possibility of social justice

As we have seen, the political liberal turn from natural rights to private property towards social justice developed out of the utilitarian tradition's distinction between production and distribution of wealth and resources. J. S. Mill famously seeks to disconnect these two components of classical political economy in his *Principles of Political Economy*.[3] His insight has been adopted by many liberals ever since, even if they have abandoned the utilitarian philosophy on which Mill's political economy was based. That said, not all post-Millian liberals have been happy with this distinction. Conservative liberal critics of social justice, such as Friedrich Hayek, have sought to reject precisely this distinction. Hayek attacks the whole agenda of contemporary liberal theories of distributive justice from a variety of directions. One of these is based on epistemological arguments against the possibility of planned economies, and is exemplified in his attack on the welfare state and nationalization in *The Road to Serfdom*.[4] He also employs a strand of argument that rests on a version of utilitarianism, to the extent that unregulated markets and freedom of property are the most beneficial and efficient ways of organizing political societies in the long run. This argument was particularly influential among the 'new right' in the 1970s and 1980s. But, most controversially for contemporary liberal theories of justice, he argues that the whole idea of 'social' justice rests upon a misunderstanding.[5] Rawls, Barry and all other liberal theorists of justice are making a basic category mistake. This is so because they assume that there is such a thing as society that can be held responsible for the overall distribution of power and resources. But this is where Hayek claims the mistake lies. Society is not a thing – or at least not a single thing – that can be ascribed agency. It is the mistake of organic, idealist and totalitarian theories of the state to think of the state or society as a single entity with a will of its own. Instead society is merely a collection of individuals with their own wills and intentions. When we speak of social injustice we are, according to Hayek, merely being inexact. This is because the overall pattern of property holdings, and the differences in income between the best and worst off, are not the result of society's decision or act of will, but rather the countless independent decisions of individuals acting in pursuit of their legitimate interests. The overall pattern of property holdings, even if grossly inegalitarian, is, according to Hayek, nobody's fault, and consequently it is incorrect to say that it gives rise to questions of justice. If Hayek is right, then much of what distinguishes contemporary political liberalism from classical liberalism disappears, and we are left with a choice between utilitarian and rights-based libertarianisms, concerned with individual liberty but not with material equality. But is he right?

As a matter of conceptual clarification it is by no means clear that a category mistake is being made. Even if one concedes Hayek's point about social ontology, and accepts that society is simply the name for the sum total of its individual members, and not some special 'metaphysical' entity that is independent of those members, it still does not follow that the idea of social justice is a category error. We might, for example, claim that political society does have a will in terms of the expression of its democratically legitimate legislative institutions. This will is manifested in law-making. Do we need to posit some account of the organic personality of the state in order to make sense of the authority of law or of our representative institutions? Yet Hayek might reply that although we can use the idea of society in this way the actual distributions of property, wealth and power in society are only the function of political institutions in totalitarian states; in all other cases they are the result of the interconnected and overlapping decisions of individuals in markets, pursuing their own interests. Unless society consciously brings about the current distribution of wealth and power, it cannot be responsible for that distribution. And if it is not responsible then no issue of justice can arise. But this, too, is not the last word, for we can ascribe responsibility to people for things that they did not intend to do, and we can ascribe responsibility to people for their omissions or non-actions. A person can be held responsible for negligence, such as 'driving without due care and attention', where her actions might result in a wholly unintentional wrong. Thus we might also say that while society, as the sum total of its members, does not intend huge disparities in income and power, it is nevertheless responsible for those disparities. Furthermore, we might also say that in so far as the political institutions of the state did nothing about those disparities then by its inactions it is willing an injustice towards those who must bear the brunt of such unequal distributions. The relevant act of will is manifested in the decisions of the political institutions of the state that express its legislative and policy-making will. If we cannot speak of society as having a will in at least this (albeit perhaps fictional) sense, then it is not clear how we explain and justify any general legal and political obligations. The denial of such obligations might appeal to anarchists, but it is hardly what Hayek intended, nor Mrs Thatcher in her famous claim that 'there is no such thing as society'. The only objection that Hayek could make to this claim is that it is inappropriate for the state to rectify such injustice because it would then have to interfere in the private property rights of individuals. But this latter argument goes beyond Hayek's critique of the mirage of social justice and depends upon a strong claim for pre-political rights to private property, of the sort we find in Locke or Nozick. Such arguments are notoriously difficult to sustain, as we see in the case of Nozick, unless one makes some contestable metaphysical assumptions about natural law. But even if they can be defended, the point is that such a defence involves substantive moral and political arguments about what justice does or does not require, and not conceptual arguments about the possibility and coherence of talk about social justice.

Rawls, Dworkin and economic justice

As with so much else in contemporary liberalism, the place to start thinking about the issue of material inequality is Rawls' *A Theory of Justice*. Rawls' idea that the subject matter of social justice is the basic structure of society poses a direct challenge to Hayekian scepticism. This focus on the basic structure that Rawls in part derives from non-liberal socialists such as Marx is, no doubt, no small cause of the suspicion that Hayek and his followers feel towards Rawls and post-Rawlsian liberalism.

The basic structure includes those institutions that shape the 'principal economic and social arrangements' of a society. In shaping a just basic structure, Rawls employs two principles of justice rather than one. The first, as we have seen in the previous chapter, distributes a set of equal basic liberties. This principle does not include freedom to dispose of private property and wealth. Such matters are covered by the second principle of justice that has two parts. The definitive statement of the second principle given in *A Theory of Justice* is as follows:

> Social and economic inequalities are to be arranged so that they are both:
> (a)   to the greatest benefit of the least advantaged, consistent with the just savings principle, and
> (b)   attached to offices and positions open to all under conditions of fair equality of opportunity.[6]

In this statement of the second principle, Rawls combines a conception of fair equality of opportunity with giving priority to the worst off, when distributing access to income and wealth. As many critics have been keen to point out, Rawls' 'difference principle' is not strictly egalitarian. For, in giving priority to the worst off, it aims to justify inequalities of resources and other economic primary goods and not to claim that these should be equally distributed. Rawls' 'prioritarianism', as it is sometimes called, is no mere after-thought or concession to 'trickle-down' economics. The idea that economic inequalities have to be justified in terms of their maximal benefit to the worst off is potentially very radical indeed; it is not simply an incentive argument to ensure only the brightest enter professions such as medicine, so that the poor have brain surgeons. By giving the worst off a veto over income inequalities, Rawls believes that he addresses the core intuition behind egalitarianism in a more direct fashion than merely equalizing resources would. In this way he hopes that his account of the basic structure has the strongest possible justification, as those who potentially do worst have the knowledge that their position is as good as it can be. Any other distribution of resources, including an equal one, would actually worsen their social position. Whether he is right or not that relativities do not matter largely turns on empirical questions of social policy, which are important to political theory but not central to our concern.[7] Much of the discussion of Rawls' 'difference principle' has turned on the question of whether it would indeed be rational for the parties in the original position behind a veil of ignorance to choose to maximize the position of the worst off, rather than to adopt a principle such as average utility. These technical issues of choice behind the veil of ignorance are important for the logic of Rawls' position, but in focusing on these we can obscure the radical way in which Rawls challenges the anti-justice arguments of classical liberals.[8] The central insight of Rawls' theory, which even those who reject his account of the difference principle accept, is the severance of the link between liberalism and some variant of natural or pre-political claims to property and wealth.

The idea of freedom and basic liberties goes to the heart of what it is to be considered a moral subject and an equal citizen, such that the denial of these liberties is a denial of equality of concern and respect. The denial of pre-political rights to property does not undermine moral status and agency despite the claims of Nozick to the contrary, unless one can establish a moral relationship between a person and her property and wealth. The reason for this is the difficulty of separating claims about desert and responsibility from claims about luck and good fortune. While classical liberals and conservatives like to link the idea of property holdings to hard work and desert, most such claims are either totally bogus or impossible to distinguish from issues of luck, whether natural or social. They are bogus in so far as most income inequalities are the result of inheritance, for which no claim of responsibility can be made: nobody deserves either wealthy or feckless grandparents, so equally nobody can be said to deserve the resulting inequalities of income and advantage. For Rawls, arguments about desert and responsibility always run up against claims about natural and social luck. It is for this reason that justice with regard to the basic structure of society is prior to claims by individuals to have deserved their wealth or unequal property holdings. We need to draw a distinction between the gifts nature has blessed us with, which may enable us to benefit more than others in the pursuit of wealth and happiness, and the structure of society which enables us to exploit those opportunities. Those who can benefit from their possession of superior intellect or physical dexterity cannot use those claims to support the fairness of their being better off, as they cannot claim, as a matter of fairness, a social system which rewards some kinds of skills more highly than others. David Beckham might well be more talented than other football players, but he cannot claim a natural right to his being wealthier than anyone else, as he does not deserve to live in a world in which the rewards for being a top football player are so great. Indeed, seventy years ago, his 'talents' would not have earned him anything like the rewards he now enjoys. The difference between then and now is a fortuitous change in society: that it is organized one way rather than another is a matter of luck until it is addressed as a matter of justice.

It should be noted here that Rawls distinguishes between social primary goods, such as income, wealth and property, and natural primary goods, such as talent, skill, dexterity and intelligence. In the case of David Beckham we cannot redistribute his natural primary goods to others, as these talents are part of who he is. We cannot take the ability to play better football from one person and distribute it fairly, but we can redistribute the consequences of those natural talents on the distribution of social primary goods. Rawls' intuitive argument, which he claims is borne out by the choice of the difference principle behind the veil of ignorance, is that the consequences of natural advantage are rendered just as long as they are coupled with access to fair, equal opportunity and are to the advantage of the worst off in society. This end is achieved by creating equal access to positions of income, influence and power, and by rendering these opportunities real by allocating each person an equal set of social primary goods, such as rights, income and wealth.

While Rawls' difference principle has been central to liberal arguments about equal treatment within liberal theory, it has also come under considerable criticism from egalitarian liberals such as Ronald Dworkin.[9] Dworkin criticizes the difference principle at the beginning of his own theory of distributive justice on the grounds that it is insufficiently 'endowment insensitive' and 'ambition sensitive'. He identifies two potential weaknesses in Rawls' theory. First, Rawls' difference principle attempts to distribute only social primary goods. But this overlooks the claims of those who are unequally endowed with natural primary goods. In particular it ignores the situation of the disabled, whose need is for more resources to compensate for unequal natural endowments. Second, the difference principle is also ambition *insensitive*. To illustrate this claim, imagine two people who are both beneficiaries of an equal distribution of primary goods and both with equal natural endowments in terms of strength and intelligence. One is a tennis player and the other a gardener. The tennis player uses his resources to support his interest in playing tennis, whereas the gardener cultivates his garden and produces beautiful flowers and vegetables, which he can enjoy and sell to others. Both make choices about how best to use their resources, but the choices of the gardener soon result in his being better off than the tennis player. The ambition-sensitive choices of each individual result in the emergence of a new pattern of distribution. However, for the new departure from the initial distribution to be justifiable in Rawlsian terms, there would have to be a transfer from the industrious gardener to the tennis player in order to justify any inequality that was emerging between them. The tennis player's lifestyle might well prove to be very expensive, so that although he gets much fulfilment from playing tennis he achieves little by way of income. The gardener also finds fulfilment from his choices, but, unlike the tennis player, under the Rawlsian scheme he finds himself having to subsidize the choices of the tennis players of society, as well as pay for his own consumption choices. Or perhaps think of someone who chooses to consume only finest clarets, compared to another who is quite happy with tea or beer. Should the person with the more frugal tastes be required to subsidize the expensive consumption choices of others?

If the Rawlsian difference principle cannot distinguish between inequalities that are the result of unequal endowments, and those that are the result of different consumption decisions or ambitions, then it runs up against the primary intuition about fairness that Rawls claims is at the heart of social justice. The reason for this is that few (though not all) political philosophers wish to deny that inequalities resulting from the expensive preferences or tastes of agents are not a matter of distributive justice.[10] If I wish to consume expensive claret and plovers' eggs then I should expect to see that consumption choice have greater impact on my income than the simpler and frugal tastes of another person has on her income. I cannot fairly claim to be disadvantaged by my choices if they are expensive, assuming of course that I could have chosen otherwise and am not strongly determined to have the preferences and desires that I do. Apart from technical issues about the specification of Rawls' account of the difference principle, the importance of Dworkin's argument for liberal attitudes to the distribution of wealth is the connection between responsibility, justice and equality.

It should, however, be pointed out here that Rawls rejects the criticism of the difference principle on the grounds of expensive tastes and lifestyles. For Rawls, the issue of responsibility and choice is completely irrelevant within the confines of a fair distribution of primary goods. As the point of the difference principle is to maintain a distribution of primary goods that secures fair equality of opportunity and is to the advantage of the worst off, the question of how a distribution comes about is irrelevant. For Rawls, to reintroduce the idea of ambition sensitivity is to make an unnecessary concession to the concepts of desert and merit. It is important to note that in connecting Dworkin's account of ambition sensitivity and endowment insensitivity to the discussion of Rawls' theory, I am not endorsing Dworkin's position as a critique of Rawls' difference principle.

If, as Dworkin claims, liberals want to argue that individuals are due equal respect, then we cannot expect some individuals to subsidize or bear the burdens of other choices. If, as liberals claim, individuals should be allowed to form and pursue their own conceptions of a good life, they must also acknowledge that individuals must accept that some of their choices cannot be cost-free. Consequently, an adequate liberal theory of justice must distinguish between inequalities of income and wealth that are a result of chance and circumstance, and those that are a result of choice. Dworkin claims we can achieve this balance between ambition sensitivity and endowment insensitivity if we adopt the idea of 'resource' egalitarianism. This is the idea that the requirement to treat others with equal concern and respect is fulfilled when we see that each has access to an equal amount of basic resources that set the parameters to their conception of the good or worthwhile life.

He illustrates this idea with a hypothetical auction for a group of people on a desert island bidding amongst each other for sets of goods with which they can pursue their chosen lives, each using an equal amount of a common currency. The occupants of the desert island each have an equal share of an otherwise valueless good – 'clamshells'. Using these, and assuming that each has different conceptions of the good life – including playing sport and cultivating one's garden – and that they have to cooperate with each other in the pursuit of their individual life plans, they all enter into a hypothetical auction.[11] The point of the auction is that people use the amount of clamshells that provide them with equal purchasing power in order to bid for sets of resources that best suit their life choices and goals. People have different life choices, so will often need different sets of resources in order to live out those goals and plans. The person with expensive tastes will need more of some resources than do others with less expensive tastes. The point is to identify a fair share of resources, given that not everyone can have everything they want all of the time, but equally, a share of resources that does not automatically privilege the choices of some over those of others. The auction allows each person to acquire precisely the set of resources that she needs, given their equal purchasing power, to pursue her own life goals. Each person should therefore prefer her own set of resources to those of anyone else. If she does prefer the set of resources of another to her own then the auction can be rerun so that she could bid for that alternative set. The auction is complete when each person has bid for her set of resources and each prefers her own set to those of anyone else. This is what Dworkin calls the envy-test.[12] However, one should bear in mind that the hypothetical auction is supposed to be dynamic so that it can be run and rerun to respond to changes in individual choices relative to those of others. The envy-test is satisfied when each person prefers her own bundle of goods to that of another – when the differences in resources between people reflects different choices about what makes life go well and different ambitions – each in effect is prepared to pay for the consequences of her own choices. In this way the tennis player purchases the bundle of resources most appropriate to his lifestyle and does not envy the resources of a gardener – as he could have bid for that set of resources himself. Thus the inequality between the two in this case is justified, as it was not under Rawls' difference principle (according to Dworkin) because it reflects the ambition-sensitive dispositions of each agent and her choices.

There are certain features to Dworkin's theory which need to be spelt out carefully. First, the distribution respects the liberal egalitarian concern with neutrality between conceptions of the good life. For Dworkin, our differing views about the good life should be reflected in our choices and not determined from the outside by the state. It is no part of the state's role to privilege any particular conception of the good. Second, the auction distinguishes between personality and personal resources. It is the latter that is the concern of distributive justice. This maintains the idea of the liberal distinction between choice and chance. We can legitimately be held responsible for our choices, whereas we cannot be held responsible for inequalities that are the result of chance or brute luck. Finally, the distribution of resources is egalitarian in the relevant sense for Dworkin because the sets of resources each person has are equal in their opportunity cost. That is, the value of the options forgone is no greater than the value of the choices I make with my own resources. The point of the auction and the envy-test is to draw attention to the relevant object of equality: what precisely we should say in response to the question 'Equality of what?'

The ambition-sensitive auction that I have just described does however assume that each participant is equal in their natural endowments, that is, their physical capacities and abilities. If this is assumed, then Dworkin's quasi-market solution to distributive justice might seem attractive. Yet the simple auction model does not capture this latter concern because it does not take account of the fact that the envy-test would not be satisfied as long as any person could claim that their bundle of resources does not reflect their choices.

Dworkin needs a way of addressing this problem of unequal natural endowments. There are some possible moves he can make to overcome this problem. First, he could argue that prior to the auction there is a distribution of social goods to compensate for natural disadvantage. Once the appropriate level of compensation is agreed the auction could be run with the remaining resources and the resulting inequalities would then reflect choice. This compensation strategy will cover some kinds of endowment deficits and allow persons to bid for resources on equal terms thereafter. But not all endowment deficits fall into this category. Those who are severely handicapped or the long-term sick will not be able to be compensated in this way by access to a fixed additional set of resources. This compensation scheme must ultimately fail because it cannot equalize the circumstances of the worst off in terms of endowment deficits. However, the whole idea of full equality of circumstance is also problematic. There seem to be two things wrong with the idea. First, it is not clear that in the most extreme cases it even makes sense to talk about equalizing the circumstances of those with the greatest endowment deficits and those who are able-bodied, so that each can pursue their own conceptions of the good on equal terms. For someone who is severely mentally retarded or physically disabled it is hard to see how any amount of resources can genuinely equalize circumstances. The best we can realistically hope for is adequate care and support to prevent suffering and improve the quality of life of that person, but that is a very different issue. Second, even if it is possible to attach a cash value to the endowment deficit and therefore try to establish equality of circumstance, this is likely to be so costly as to leave little or nothing to enable others to act on the basis of their choices. Here we would have a case of the able-bodied and equally endowed being the virtual servants of those with endowment deficits. This would turn the dependency of the most disabled on its head by making the able-bodied person's ability to pursue her own life conditional on the claims of the disabled. This is also a form of injustice or unfairness by denying the equal value of life options. So, while we have an obligation to the worst off in these cases, that obligation cannot be to eradicate the full effects of circumstances in our account of a just distribution.

To address this problem, Dworkin adopts the device of a hypothetical insurance scheme.[13] This scheme is designed to identify the level of social provision that we are prepared to support in order to compensate for natural disadvantages and endowment deficits. This is a second-best solution because it cannot fully compensate for the effects of circumstance and endowment deficit, and because it means we cannot provide a pure account of a just distribution that is genuinely endowment-insensitive and ambition-sensitive. However, Dworkin believes it tends towards that position and is therefore the best we can hope for.

The hypothetical insurance scheme works in the following way. We should imagine ourselves behind a modified veil of ignorance, where we know certain things, but we do not know our place in the distribution of natural talents. Furthermore, we assume that we are equally susceptible to the variety of natural disadvantages that might arise in the future. When we are given our equal allocation of clamshells, we are asked how much we would be prepared to spend on insurance against being handicapped or disadvantaged in respect of endowments. If people decide that it would be reasonable to spend twenty-five of their clamshells on insurance against natural disadvantage this can be used as a guide for public provision of support through the taxation system.

The hypothetical contract device does not give us a specific answer to the appropriate level of compensation but it does model how we might decide the appropriate level of compensation. However, this is not a one-off form of compensation, as we saw in the attempt to compensate prior to the auction. The other crucial feature of the insurance scheme is that it connects the issue of compensation for natural disadvantage with choice by assuming that it is irrational for anyone to fail to provide some level of compensation against natural disadvantage, but acknowledging that it is equally irrational to spend all of one's resources on compensation against disadvantage. Like Rawls' conception of the original position, the point of the hypothetical insurance scheme is to model a fair solution for the problem of compensation to those with endowment deficits.

The combination of the hypothetical auction and the hypothetical insurance scheme is designed to provide a theory of distributive justice, which treats people as equals and is ambition-sensitive and endowment-insensitive. Dworkin's theory is the most influential liberal theory of justice in its attempt to combine considerations of fairness and equality with choice and responsibility. Dworkin does not use the Rawlsian language of the basic structure of society, but he is concerned, as are all liberals, with the fair background conditions in which individuals find themselves and in which they have to pursue their life choices. However, alongside that concern with a fair basic structure or set of background conditions, he endorses the liberal view that overall outcomes should reflect the choices and actions of individuals. This commitment has a resonance beyond Dworkin's own theory and has come to define the debate between liberal and non-liberal egalitarians.

Distinguishing between choice and chance

Dworkin's own theory has inspired considerable criticism that centres around how one is to turn his modified hypothetical auction into a set of institutions that can deliver liberal egalitarian justice. Yet his approach has also inspired a more fundamental set of criticisms that address the distinction between choice and chance that is at the heart of liberalism. Marxist-inspired philosophers such as G. A. Cohen, and multiculturalists such as Will Kymlicka, have been at the forefront of challenging the Dworkinian distinction between choice and chance, or luck and responsibility, thus making the whole liberal egalitarian approach to economic justice incoherent.[14] In the remainder of this chapter I will examine that critique and what liberals say in defence of the distinction.

Cohen's argument denies the possibility of a simple contrast between choice and chance. Instead, he distinguishes between outcomes that are voluntarily chosen and those that are the result of brute luck. He differs from liberal egalitarians in where he draws the line between choice and brute luck, arguing that an individual's ambition-sensitive dispositions are often themselves matters of luck or chance. Aspects of our personality, such as our propensity to work hard or our academic ability, are at least in part shaped by inheritance. Thus, if we are disadvantaged in the labour market by our inability to obtain high-skilled and high-paid employment, this might not be seen as fair even if it is the result of poor performance at school. Genetic inheritance is not the only relevant factor. Some, perhaps all, of our ambition-sensitive dispositions are the result of socialization. If one has been brought up in a context that devalues many of the skills necessary for superior economic achievement in society, then that too might be a ground for redistribution as individuals cannot be responsible for their socialization. Consequently, the grounds of choice themselves become a matter of luck, and therefore we potentially have reason to compensate for all inequalities, however they arise. Unless we actually choose to have and cultivate expensive preferences, then we can claim compensation for the inequalities that arise from having them. If I just have the preferences of a lazy 'couch potato' through no choice of my own then I cannot be said to deserve to be worse off than someone else who is lucky enough to be born with an ambitious and hard-working disposition. Such a view would involve the abandonment of the liberal aspiration to justify fair inequalities and a move towards a more straightforward conception of equality.

Multiculturalists such as Will Kymlicka make a similar argument that cultural identity and affiliation is also not strictly chosen. Hence, those in minority cultures who find their lifestyle highly costly in relation to the wider society's norms are able to claim compensation, to sustain special schooling or minority languages. This seems to be a classic case of the requirement for some people to subsidize the life choices and preferences of others, although Kymlicka is at pains to claim that this approach is perfectly consistent with liberal egalitarianism.[15]

Can liberalism retain a commitment to the distinction between choice and chance in the face of these criticisms? Dworkin has recently set out to salvage the crucial basis of the liberal account of justice. The first argument he deploys is based on an account of our ordinary understanding of morality and is designed to answer the challenge that because the expensiveness of a preference is a matter of luck, people should not be expected to deserve inequalities that result from their having expensive tastes. Similarly, because our tastes are also not something that we choose, we should not be penalized because we have what turn out to be expensive tastes.

His response depends upon a distinction between forms of luck. Dworkin distinguishes between those forms of luck that raise issues of fairness and those forms of luck (which Matravers calls cosmic luck) that do not.[16] In one sense, we might speak of luck in terms of things turning out one way rather than another. So we might say it is a matter of chance that the planet Earth satisfies the conditions of life in the universe, in order to draw a contrast with divine purpose. But such a judgement is generally morally neutral; in itself the fact that the solar system has the character that it does is a matter of chance, but whether this is a good thing or not is another question. It would be rather odd to say that it is a matter of bad luck that the planet is not different from the way it is. No issue of fairness arises. On the other hand, we might say that while it is also a matter of chance (good or bad luck) that I am born into a particular social position, it is not the case that this rules out issues of fairness. Understood in this way, Dworkin thinks he can address Cohen's concerns about the expensiveness of tastes and preferences relative to those of others. Thus, while I find myself in a world within which certain tastes and preference are considered more expensive because of the free decisions of others, this kind of chance is not the kind that can be considered either fair or unfair, as long as we all begin from a fair baseline of resources. That we place the distinction between inequalities that are the result of choice, and those that are the result of chance, against a prior baseline of equality is precisely what Dworkin and other 'semi-choicist' liberals such as Brian Barry claim.

This distinction between kinds of luck is supposed to clarify the issue between choice and chance by putting the issue of responsibility for tastes and preferences beyond the scope of the distinction. It is supported by an appeal to ordinary morality. This is an appeal to our common-sense intuitions about where we see consequential responsibility residing: that is, when should individuals bear the burdens of their situations? We need the distinction between choice and chance to preclude some of the bizarre consequences of compensating for tastes, preferences and dispositions. Should a constitutionally boring person have a claim for compensation because he has no friends or life partner? After all, if they cannot help being boring do they deserve to have no friends? Liberals clearly think that such issues fall foul of our conventional moral intuitions about fairness and responsibility. They also challenge the liberals' core belief that individuals are in some special sense responsible for their own lives and should be left alone by the state and society to decide the content of a good life for themselves. The appeal to intuitions will do some work, as any account of responsibility has to achieve some kind of reflective equilibrium with our basic concepts and commitments. But that appeal must be cautious, as most often our intuitions are uncertain (that is after all why we have the activity of political theory!). The appeal to intuition can try and show what is at stake in abandoning some interpretations in favour of others, but it cannot settle conflicts.

Liberals need a stronger argument if Cohen's critique is not to undermine the choice versus chance distinction. Dworkin attempts to provide this argument by considering the way in which we identify with, or endorse, our choices and preferences.[17] He illustrates the point by distinguishing between two cases. The first involves a man who finds the taste of tap water unbearably sour and therefore has to spend more of his resources on bottled water. The second is of a person who finds himself with the ambition to be a photographer. Again, the second person did not choose this preference but merely found himself with it and the consequent need to buy expensive equipment. Both cases do not assume that the agents choose their preferences, but they relate to them in very different ways. In the case of the first person, we might well say that his tastes are just brute bad luck and that finding ordinary tap water unbearably sour just is a misfortune, unless we were then to imagine a hypothetical situation in which the person were offered a pill to change his taste for tap water; in this case the person has a choice and is no longer the victim of brute bad luck. However, in the second case, although the original aspiration was also not chosen, Dworkin argues that the person's relationship to his expensive taste is much more complex. This is the argument from identification. In this latter case our expensive preference forms part of an interconnected web of beliefs and judgements about what things have value to us. In this way the preference, though not chosen, is partly endorsed by being implicated in this web of judgement, value and what one takes a good life to mean. Many of our preferences and tastes are not discrete in the way in which the taste for water might be; therefore, according to Dworkin, we are more likely to endorse their featuring in our conception of what matters to us. If this is so, then the photographer is less likely to take a pill to change his preferences just because they involve expense, for that would involve eradicating something that is central to his personality. If the photographer is unwilling to make this choice then there is something strange about the claim that he finds his preference for photography a matter of brute bad luck for which he should be compensated.

The point about this distinction is that it enables the liberal to claim that if one is prepared to endorse a lifestyle that involves a complex web of preferences, each of which we did not choose but that we value, then we cannot claim to be unjustly treated if living that life makes us worse off relative to others because that web of preferences turns out to be expensive. Dworkin's distinction is by no means uncontroversial, but then neither is Cohen's alternative account of where one should divide choice from chance, as his distinction would in effect allow very little to count as choice. Yet the fact that Cohen's preferred account is more burdensome is no argument against his criticism of where Dworkin draws the distinction. Some commentators have claimed that Dworkin's distinction is unsustainable, as is the liberal's attempt to do political theory without metaphysics; there is no alternative but to provide a full theory of freedom and responsibility.[18]

But that does not mean that Dworkin's position is without any force, nor does it mean that liberals must seek a philosophical theory of responsibility. Dworkin's argument turns on the liberal idea that endorsement is central to any account of why individuals should be free to form and pursue their own conceptions of what makes life go well. The endorsement constraint underlies appeals to the value of freedom and autonomy, in the weak sense that modern liberals use. Yet there is indeed something curious about the idea that we can be said to endorse the complex of preferences and judgements we make about what makes a life go well, and yet reject the consequences of those preferences and judgements. The reason for this is that the relative values attached to particular preferences and choices are a function of the different individual choices that people make with their resources. One cannot abandon the idea that choices should have consequences without also undermining the liberal claim that the value of the good life is something that the state and wider society must leave to the individual. To say that those consequences are unfair because they result in differential outcomes is to miss the point at which the issue of fairness really arises. This for Dworkin is at the prior level at which we distinguish the fair economic baseline in terms of resources that allow for broadly equal opportunity sets. What neither Dworkin nor any liberal is arguing is the familiar conservative claim, that the poor or worst off are responsible for their position because of the choices they make. To assume that this is the liberal position is to ignore the whole point of equalizing resources as a way of establishing a fair baseline, from which people can be said to endorse their lifestyles. As long as the opportunity sets are of the same value, and individuals are not forced to make only one choice within those sets, then it is not unreasonable to hold them responsible for the overall level of resources relative to others. Indeed, to try and do otherwise would involve presupposing the truth about controversial theories of the personality and free will and responsibility: theories which show that we are not responsible for our personalities, character or any of the choices we make. Or, more troubling still, it might leave us challenging the liberal claim that individuals can genuinely endorse or choose forms of life that others regard as foolish or demeaning.

One consequence of setting the issue of choice against the backdrop of a fair baseline distribution is that it has the potentially radical implication of significantly narrowing the justifiable differences in wealth and resources. After all, justified inequalities have to be shown to be the result of choices within a system of equal resource sets, and this is unlikely to sanction anything like the huge differentials of income and power that we currently find in modern societies.

That still leaves the question of the justification of the distinction, but it clarifies its implication for a liberal account of social justice. Responsibility does not contradict the claims of fairness, but is perfectly compatible with it. Yet to abandon the distinction altogether is to undermine a concept that has wide use beyond issues of distributive justice such as punishment. Some liberal theorists have explicitly turned to legal theory to show how the idea of responsibility as a set of justifiable excuses, in the way deployed by H. L. A. Hart in his theory of punishment, can allow us to use the concept without resort to complex metaphysical questions. Hart suggests that we can learn a lot about ascriptions of responsibility from one of the social practices in which the concept is most important, namely liability to punishment in the legal system.[19] The justificatory approach here is to assume responsibility as a background condition and identify excusing conditions when it might be said not to hold or be diminished. Only in special circumstances would diminished responsibility be said to hold, otherwise as long as individuals have a realistic course of action open to them they can be held responsible for their choices. This view of responsibility fits with the liberal idea of equal opportunity sets and alternative courses of action. Once these background conditions of justice obtain, individuals can be said to deserve the resulting inequalities that emerge from their life choices, unless they really have no alternative or are unable to act. The fact that one finds an alternative life choice more burdensome than another, because of one's beliefs and values, does not prevent that option from being a genuine alternative. Those who seek to pursue minority lifestyles cannot expect to find them without burden. That said, in first seeking to equalize opportunity sets, liberals already undercut the claim that people do not deserve the economic position that is associated with any particular life choice. What liberals do not allow is the fact that the risky, expensive or dangerous lifestyles should be subsidized by the rest of society. If people wish to use their resources pursuing particularly dangerous sports, they can hardly claim an unfairness if they are required to pay higher insurance premiums, or enjoy a lower level of income as a result. To offer a full comparison between Hart's excuse theory and full metaphysical theories of free will and responsibility would take us too far beyond the boundaries of liberal theory. The important point for liberal theory is to show that the choice versus chance distinction can be upheld and that it does not involve a retreat to the pre-Rawlsian view that responsibility undermines the egalitarianism of liberal theories of justice.

The point of the discussion in this chapter has been to show why liberals do not regard wealth and property as prepolitical rights which preclude social justice and equalizing opportunities over time. The rather arcane and specialized debates that result can often lead students to regard liberal theory as wholly divorced from reality. After all, if Rawls' veil of ignorance was complex, how much more complex was Dworkin's discussions of auctions involving clamshells and hypothetical insurance markets? How can one use Dworkin's ideas in policy-making? If they cannot be institutionalized are they worth taking seriously? Finally, how do these questions relate to the real world of supply-side economics? It's all well and good discussing ever more complex distributional questions, but what happens about economic globalization and the pressures of global capitalism?

It is important, by way of conclusion, to make clear what this kind of theory is for. It is not, as Hayek and others might sometimes claim, the utopian fantasizing of rationalist philosophers who are cocooned from the real economy. Certainly, Dworkin, Rawls and Barry all hope that their theories might give some direction to the public policies of the societies in which they find themselves. Their conclusions point in a clear direction on matters such as tax rates. But they also serve a more important purpose, and that is to demolish the claims of many that the wealthiest in society deserve their good fortune as a reward for hard work or talent, and therefore that taxation for redistribution is just the politics of envy. Whatever else these liberal theories can do, they can certainly show that these claims are bogus and self-serving. In the end we may be stuck, for pragmatic reasons, with a greater level of economic inequality than liberal theories justify. But at least we can be clear about the reasons for these inequalities and we have the resources to challenge those who claim that the rich and powerful either merit their position or have a right to it.

6

How Political is Political Liberalism?

The previous chapters have provided us with an account of the origins and nature of contemporary liberalism as a political doctrine. We have seen how it draws key ideas from both the contractualist and utilitarian traditions. We have also seen that in its contemporary guise it develops the idea of a political community as a fair system of social cooperation, or an impartially ordered basic institutional structure of society. This impartialist or fair basic structure is shaped by two considerations of distributive justice. First, by an equal system of basic liberties; and second, by a basic distribution of resources that reflects as closely as possible choices of individuals in living their lives, and which rules out inequalities that are the result of luck or misfortune. In this way a liberal political order sets out a conception of the political community within which individuals can be regarded as free and equal, and responsible for the ultimate shape of their own lives. People are not told by the state how they should live their lives, and the state limits its responsibilities to conformity with these two person-regarding constraints on politics and policy. Remember, that in defending this vision of the state as a fair system of social cooperation, liberal theory does not claim that there are no objective goods. It merely asserts the nature and limits to which state and political power can be exercised over individuals. Political liberalism, properly understood, is not a consequence of epistemological limitations, but involves a moral limitation on the exercise of coercive power over those who are of equal moral status. Different liberal theorists, such as Rawls or Barry, either refuse to be drawn, or remain agnostic about the wider status of morality and ethical value. Political liberalism is political precisely because it confines its attention to what it regards as the political domain and does not attempt to colonize the whole of the public realm with morality. Although political liberalism is ubiquitous in contemporary political theory, to the extent that it is often identified with political theory itself, it is a highly controversial doctrine, and in the next three chapters I will focus on different objections to it. In the next chapter we will address the issue of false neutrality and the ethnocentricity of this liberal conception of the political. In a later chapter we will also look at the connection of this idea with a narrow juridical conception of the sovereign state. In that chapter we will discuss how political liberalism fares in the light of the transformation of the state under the pressures of multicultural disaggregation on the one hand, and globalization on the other. In this chapter I want to address a much more basic question, namely, whether political liberalism is actually *political* at all. This may seem a curious question, but some important recent critics of political liberalism have argued that it not only misunderstands the nature of politics, but actually tries to displace politics altogether.

This argument has been advanced most recently and forcefully by, amongst others, John Gray, Glen Newey, Bonnie Honig and Chantal Mouffe.[1] It is not a particularly new criticism in that it draws on ideas from anti-liberal thinkers as diverse as Michael Oakeshott and Carl Schmitt,[2] but it has a peculiar contemporary resonance among those who aspire to cultivate what is called an *agonistic* politics. These arguments matter because they are used to claim that liberal political theory is actually anti-political in important respects and therefore fails in its own terms. At its most far-reaching the argument advanced by Gray and Newey applies to all forms of normative political theory, not only those which take their lead from John Rawls. As I take the activity of normative political theory to be important, and as I think that some variant of liberal egalitarianism is the most appealing substantive approach to normative political theory, it matters that liberal political theory is *political* in the relevant sense. But what is that?

In responding to this challenge I do not propose to give a general theory or stipulative definition of the concept of the political. Rather, my argument will turn that charge against those who wish to legislate liberal theory outside the category of political theory. In defending normative theory, and especially political liberalism, in this way, I do not wish to claim that they constitute all there is to political theory – and this is an important point, although not one I take to be a serious concession to Gray, Newey, Honig or Mouffe. The point of their criticism is not one about the narrowness of scope of contemporary liberal political theory. Newey and Gray think that the scope of much that goes under the guise of political theory *is* too narrow. In that, they follow others such as John Dunn, who has spent much of his career lamenting the narrowness of what goes for modern political theory, of almost any kind – except the history of political thought which is not narrow enough in scope. For Dunn, its 'absurd overemphasis on distributive justice' shows a 'quite ludicrous level of misjudgement' that renders political theory largely vacuous and lacking in broad intellectual relevance beyond those who are simply concerned with problems from Rawls, as others are interested in chess problems or crosswords.[3] However the issue of scope is easily rectifiable and many of those who currently practise political theory are indeed interested in, and aware of, what goes on in the wider field of political and social science. The real charge against political liberalism goes much further than this, in that it claims liberalism actually misunderstands the nature of politics, and as a result seeks to displace real politics altogether. It is this issue that I will address in this chapter – my concern is primarily with whether it is a genuine issue at all and therefore a serious objection to political liberalism.

The displacement and rejection of politics

What is wrong with the familiar picture of political liberalism outlined in the previous chapters? Some recent critics have argued that it is not only narrow in scope (an issue on which many liberal political theorists would be inclined to agree), but that it is also anti-political as it aims to tame and dispense with what is distinctive about politics. Consequently, contemporary liberal political theory can tell us very little of interest or value about politics – it is a redundant activity, which has no bearing on politics itself. In this respect liberal theory is different from the approaches taken to politics by the great thinkers from the past history of political theory, such as Aristotle or Hobbes. Far from providing a return to grand theory, the turn towards normative theorizing that is attributed to Rawls, but that encompasses Habermas as well, is a rejection of the legacy of classical political thought. This negative argument is advanced by, among others, John Gray and Chantal Mouffe, who draw on the idea of pluralism and incommensurability, and Bonnie Honig, who defends the ineradicability of political contestation; but it has been advanced most forcefully recently by Glen Newey. Newey is sympathetic to the critique of liberal political theory found in much of Gray's work, but goes further still, arguing that Gray too does not fully appreciate the way in which even a thin normative theory like political liberalism involves the denial of politics. I will therefore focus primarily on Newey's arguments, as these are the most demanding variant of the critique. If his argument fails, then the whole thesis fails and we are left with only the uncontentious claims about the scope of contemporary liberal theory, such as those advanced by Dunn or Bhikhu Parekh.[4]

In his book *After Politics*, a title which is supposed to suggest the appropriate place for political theorizing – that is, as an activity subordinate to and dependent upon the activity of politics – Glen Newey mounts a sustained assault on the pretensions of normative liberal political theory. Newey argues that the activity of modern liberal political theory is unhelpful in political philosophy's true task of the systematic reflection on things 'political'.

He begins with a distinction between political theory and political philosophy. For many political theorists there is no hard and fast distinction between the two activities: political theory is merely political philosophy when it is taught in a political science department, whereas political philosophy is political theory taught in a philosophy department. Instead, Newey wants to claim that political philosophy is of a different order from what passes for philosophy under the guise of normative political theory. In this respect political philosophy is a second-order activity concerned with conceptual distinctions, criteria and the bases of knowledge that we deploy when we do first-order normative theorizing about issues like justice and the terms of political association. Although he does not explicitly acknowledge the debt, this conception of political theorizing is clearly similar to and influenced by the Oakeshottian distinction between political philosophy, which is the systematic analysis of a mode of experience and the specific mode of practice, which is concerned with what we should do.[5] Unlike Oakeshott, Newey does not want to be so restrictive in terms of what has intellectual respectability and therefore deserves a place in the university curriculum, but he does share with Oakeshott the familiar hostility to the idea of a practically oriented philosophy, as this is indistinguishable from mere ideological advocacy. In order to overcome this tendency, political theory needs to be less focused on normativity or what is to be done, and much more focused on a systematic analysis of politics as it is. Rather like critics such as John Dunn, Newey claims that political theory needs to be more political by focusing on the realities of politics, rather than with what ought to be but does not yet exist. The great political thinkers of the past, such as Aristotle, did not confine their attention to normative questions, but instead ranged over descriptive and analytical reflections on the world of politics as they found it. In making this argument, Newey is not simply arguing that political philosophers should read more political science. Instead, he is arguing that political philosophy should encompass both the descriptive and normative, and direct its attention as much to analysing the concepts and categories that underpin contemporary political science as to normative concepts such as justice, liberty and equal treatment. So far the issue still seems to be one of scope, but Newey uses this indifference to the descriptive aspects of the study of politics to extend his argument further towards the claim that contemporary political theory involves the denial of politics.

A proper descriptively rooted political philosophy would be more sensitive to what the domain of the political actually is. Contemporary political liberalism and perhaps all normative theory seem remarkably indifferent to what politics as an activity actually is. But what is politics? Newey offers an account of politics that he takes to be uncontentious but still problematic for liberal political thought. This uncontroversial account of politics has three components.

Politics is characterized by endemic disagreement about what constitutes actually politics. Thus the question 'what is politics' is actually a deeply contested issue, as can be seen from the multiplicity of things covered by what is often called the history of political thought. Presumably by this claim Newey is alluding to the range of debates that challenge the idea of where politics itself resides. Feminists famously argue that 'the personal is political', in order to broaden the range of issues that should be subject to collective determination or accountability, just as anti-feminist traditionalists wish to put certain spheres, such as the family, beyond the scope of politics. Multiculturalists, such as Parekh, challenge the hegemony of the juridical state, and claim that traditional liberal approaches to issues of cultural accommodation are too state-centred in their dealings with alternative claims to authority and responsibility.[6] Is politics just about the state and what it does to those within its jurisdiction? Perhaps the recent growth of interest in issues of global justice or international distributive justice is a recognition that the Rawlsian paradigm is too state-centred and that politics does not end at the frontiers of the state: we shall return to precisely this question in the final chapter. The narrowness and controversy surrounding the conception of the political underpinning political liberalism are no doubt serious matters and worth more attention.

The second feature of politics is that, even within the realm of things that we have identified as political, there remains endemic disagreement. Here the issue is less with the scope of the concept of the political and more with the idea of disagreement itself as an irreducible factor in making politics possible and necessary. Thus, while we might agree that the state should be ordered as a fair system of social cooperation, there remains great scope for disagreement about what that entails and who should do what under such a conception. Any conception of the common good, or those things which we pursue in common (the *commonwealth*), involves dis- agreements about who gets what, and who gives what: which individuals are responsible for acting and which individuals are required to refrain from acting? This fact of disagreement goes to the heart of the defence of the state as a possible arbiter, as we find set out in different ways in Hobbes or Locke. Politics is about the irreducibility of disagreement, and that is why we need it, otherwise we could have anarchy – a world in which interest, desires, claims of need and individ- ual freedom are all naturally self-regulating. Disagreement also goes to the heart of the ranking of goods that all distributive approaches to politics are concerned with. How important is liberty in relation to equality? And, even if we can identify rankings of particular goods that fall within the remit of what we all accept as the common or public inter- est, we can still find disagreement about the determinate scope of those goods.

Even if liberty has priority over equality, this does not remove the possibility of further disagreement over the scope and ranking of particular liberties. John Gray makes much of this sort of indeterminacy in his critique of liberal politi- cal thought.[7] Like Newey, Gray's argument is that this irreducibility of disagreement is either ignored or denied by liberal political theorists. An extension of the same argument is central to Bonnie Honig's critique of political liberalism. Honig argues that politics has its roots in the irreducible con- flict of interests, and that liberal attempts to overcome those conflicts simply diverts them from one particular terrain to another. Thus, the liberals' familiar recourse to the discourse of rights does not eradicate conflict, but merely forces it on to another terrain where it remanifests itself, in such things as constitutional adjudication and the choice of Supreme Court Justices. The problem with this strategy, according to Honig, is that it is itself merely a further manifestation of the exercise of power, but one that distorts the interests at stake.[8] This brings us to the final feature of Newey's account of politics.

The final feature of politics is that it is about the use of power. Power is the one aspect of politics that appears to be lost through preoccupation with the normative at the expense of the descriptive. Normative liberal theory is concerned with questions of what ought to be the case, but in focusing on these questions it ignores the issue of why, whatever the case is, is the case? Political theory does not take seriously an account of the sources, distribution and manifestations of power in politics, nor does it take seriously the fact that the exercise of power is essential in order to deliver what one might want to be the case. The point here is not simply a matter of oversight. The point is not that liberal theories ignore a theorization of the sources of power, but rather that they ignore the fact that politics is not simply about power, as it involves the exercise of power, and the exercise of power is a dirty or ambiguous business fuelled by contingency.

Different aspects of this account of the concept of politics already open up questions about the adequacy of political liberalism. But this is only part of Newey's critique of the anti-political nature of liberal political theory. He uses this relatively uncontroversial account of politics to advance the following criticisms of liberal theory, namely that it is reductionist, instrumentalist and that it denies the autonomy of the political. And it is these characteristics of contemporary liberal political theory that make it anti-political and divorce it from the real world of politics.

Reductivism

What is distinctive about liberal normative political theory is that it sees itself as a branch of ethics or moral theory. Normative political theory is concerned with a set of questions rooted in the peculiar conception of morality that preoccupies moral philosophers. Most liberal political theorists write within a moral paradigm, and are concerned with issues such as the scope and subject of obligations: who ought to have which particular rights and liberties and who should bear the corresponding duties? The whole preoccupation of contemporary liberal theory with distributive justice, which John Dunn sees as absurd and 'ludicrously' misjudged, is simply an example of this. Moral philosophers colonize an area of enquiry and bend it towards their particular discipli-

nary concerns. These concerns are normative (covering obligation, duty, right, liberty, etc.), and this explains the relative
indifference of political theorists to the traditionally more
descriptive concerns of political philosophy, with its systematic reflection on the nature of things political in the sense
given above regarding the general conception of the nature
of politics. The failing of this approach is not simply that it
misconstrues the activity of politics, although that is serious
enough, rather, it is that such misconstrual actually undermines the value of what an overly moralized conception of
politics is supposed to deliver. According to Newey, the
reductivist approach 'offers simplification, by showing that
one subject-matter can be translated, without remainder into
another. But this can only seem possible given an over-
simplified view of the original subject matter.'[9] By reducing
the diversity of politics to the issues of ethics and morality,
liberal political theory loses a sense of what is political. It narrowly addresses certain distributive questions, because it can,
but it inadequately addresses these questions because it sim-
plifies the diversity of manifestations of power and agency
into individualistic claims to right and recognition. Newey
argues that liberal political theory illustrates this problem in
its recognition of both the fact of reasonable pluralism, and
the relative ease with which normative theorists proceed to
dispense with that inconvenient fact when constructing ideas
such as reasonable consent or endorsement, as the basis for
the distribution of rights and responsibilities. In this handling
of the problem of the pluralism of conceptions of the good,
liberal political theory appears to ignore not only the true
character of fundamental disagreement, but also its bases
and, more importantly, what would be necessary to deal with
it over time. Liberal theory deploys an implausible conception of agency, but what is more it seems to do so at its con-
venience. Yet, unless liberal theory is able to provide both an
adequate response to the problem of radical disagreement
about fundamental ends and about the prospects of sustaining mechanisms for dealing with this issue, its arguments
remain irrelevant. It manages to appear to deal with this
problem only because it attempts to dispense with contingency, in order to provide us with a world of order and principle. But, as the world of politics remains a peculiarly

Machiavellian world in which contingency reigns, the retreat to a Kantian world beyond contingency, that liberal political theory is supposed to offer, is actually a retreat from the political.

The reductivist turn of normative liberalism is the basis for the denial of politics and a ground for the redundancy of normative political theory. But reductivism is not the only problem with contemporary liberal political theory. Connected to the idea of reductivism and the displacement of politics by morality, is the instrumentalization of liberal politics.

Instrumentalism

By reducing politics to the subject matter of ethics or morality, liberal political theory also introduces a further problem regarding its own pretensions to adequacy. This is so because the dominant strands of moral thinking that underpin liberal political theory are themselves primarily instrumentalist about ends. In this charge, Newey reflects Alasdair MacIntyre's claims about the utilitarian character of the emotivist culture of liberal modernity.[10] Newey sets out the issue of intrumentalism as follows:

> Political instrumentalism holds, that politics exists to serve ends that are prior to and external to it, and that political deliberation raises no special problems not to be found in individual practical reasoning.
> Instrumentalism implies a certain relationship between political activity and civil society . . . The implied relationship is that politics merely fills two complementary roles – negatively, to referee civil society conflicts when they occur, and positively, to facilitate the pursuit of civil society interests or conceptions of the good by using appropriate managerial techniques. As a result philosophical reflection on politics is attenuated, or transformed into something else.[11]

The emphasis on managerialism certainly reflects concerns similar to those of MacIntyre.[12] However, there are some other important aspects of Newey's critique revealed in the above quotation. The reduction of politics to morality has a tendency to individualize the ends that politics is supposed to be concerned with, as liberal political theory endorses nor-

mative individualism in either its deontological or conse-
quentialist guises. But more than this, it also sees the task of
theory solely as the arbitration of individual conceptions of
the good. These conceptions of the good are either highly
moralized, and refer to comprehensive moralities or theo-
logies (as liberal political theory still functions under the long
shadow of seventeenth-century debates about religious
toleration), or else they are a redescription of individual
wants or preferences. For MacIntyre, the former actually
collapse into the latter due to the consequences of secular-
ization. The important feature of preferences or wants is that
they are supposed to be brute facts or the basis for practical
reasoning, and not subject to further deliberation. In this way
wants and preferences are pre-given and prior to the activity
of politics. Liberal political theory then becomes the search
for the appropriate procedure for managing the most efficient
pursuit of pre-political ends. Politics as we find it in liberal
political thought is therefore a subset of ethics concerned with
the means to achieve pre-given *apolitical* individualistic ends.

This 'instrumental' vision of political theory creates two
problems for political liberalism. First, by removing the issue
of ends or goals from the sphere of politics, liberal political
theory distorts both the nature and character of those ends
and the mechanisms through which those ends are achieved.
Liberalism is preoccupied with the idea of reasonable compromise between equals. Yet, according to Newey, this is to
beg the question by imposing a finite and ideal set of higher-
order motivations on political agents that have little basis in
the real world of political action and struggle. Again, the
attempt to discipline politics has the consequences of undermining precisely what liberal theory needs in order to address
political disagreement. Second, the preoccupation with pre-
political and essentially individualized ends, that we find in
normative political theory, precludes the possibility of exploring the extent to which contemporary liberal political theory
is dominated by the structures and problems of our ordinary
domestic politics at the expense of less individualized ends,
such as group identity, class, or other group interests. In this
way liberal political theory is normalized by having its agenda
set by extra-political forces that can include either the

dominant conceptions of the liberal democratic state, or more worryingly the narrow preoccupations of a hierarchically organized academic discipline.[13] This tendency to shy away from politics, and the politics of political theory itself, is further reinforced, according to Newey, by the generally low esteem in which contemporary liberal political theorists hold politicians.

The charges of reductivism and instrumentalism both assume a further feature of Newey's argument, namely, the autonomy of the political. This is an idea that he shares with many radical political theorists, such as Chantal Mouffe and other theorists of an agonistic politics.[14] The idea of the autonomy of politics, or the 'political' as it is often referred to, has a number of sources, not least perhaps Thomas Hobbes. But it is most famously associated with the German political thinker Carl Schmitt.[15] Schmitt is famous for many things, not all of which are to his credit, but perhaps most famously he is responsible for recovering the autonomy of the political from the tyranny of liberalism, and his assertion of the friend–enemy distinction as the site of politics. Schmitt writes: 'liberal concepts typically move between ethics (intellectuality) and economics (trade). From that polarity they [liberals] attempt to annihilate the political as a domain of conquering power and repression.'[16] Schmitt is important to critics of liberalism such as Mouffe and Newey because he calls attention to the ineradicable conflictual character of politics itself. This is not merely a rejection of what is often considered the mundane character of ordinary liberal politics. Schmitt's plea for the autonomy of politics is a call for a brutal realism that recognizes what is actually at the heart of politics, namely conflict. By failing to take seriously the reality and ineradicability of conflict, liberal political theory not only fails to be political, but, more importantly, undermines its own aspirations to tame politics and bend it to reason.

If Newey and the radical critics who he draws upon are correct, then failing to be political does not merely require liberalism to seek a new designation, but has a bearing on the activity itself. The question, of course, is whether he is right.

Legislating for political theory – political liberalism defended

One simple response to Newey would be to show that he offers a rather strained stipulative definition of politics, and that if we define it rather differently then political liberalism comes through with flying colours or at least substantially unscathed. In part that is what I propose to argue, but not quite so simply: that is because Newey raises important points about the preoccupations of contemporary liberal political theorists. The issue is whether these are points against the unduly narrow scope of contemporary liberal political theory, or whether these do show that political liberalism denies politics altogether. If the former is the case then liberal theory can simply accommodate these points and broaden its scope. I am inclined to this view, but why?

Much of the force of Newey's reductivist and intrumentalist critique trades on the persuasiveness of the 'autonomy' of the political. To support the idea that there is something wrong in the idea of at least establishing a continuity between ethics and politics (an idea that is after all found in Aristotle), and that the liberal conception of politics relies on external pre-political goods, we need to presuppose the idea of politics as an autonomous sphere with its own unique goods. But what is the argument for this view? At worst, as with Mouffe, it is just asserted and then backed up with a quotation from Schmitt. Schmitt's own argument is less simplistic, but even that is based on some quite controversial philosophical assumptions, not least the assertion of a form of ethical nihilism. Newey's own view is not explicitly Schmittian and seems to draw more heavily on Oakeshottian ideas about distinct orders of experience. Oakeshott quite explicitly presents an account of philosophy as a second-order activity, concerned with mapping or distinguishing different orders of experience. In order for one mode to be what it is, it has to be categorically distinguished from any other. Politics as part of the mode of practical experience has to be distinguished from history or science and, indeed, from philosophy, which has no substantive content. The Oakeshottian view gives us an account of philosophy as a contentless reflection on the order of experience, so in that sense there cannot be any political philosophy as such – there is only philosophy. Political philosophy (in so far as it exists) is really just philosophy reflecting on the presuppositions of practice, or engaged practical experience (as such, political philosophy is more like the history of ideas than normative political theory) – 'Everything is what it is and not another thing'.[17] This approach gives us a possible ground for distinguishing the autonomy of a mode of experience, but Oakeshott gives us the whole of practical experience and not merely politics as such. So this approach needs to be supplemented by Newey in order to give us an account of the autonomy of the political that distinguishes it from the ethical and other forms of practical experience. Newey needs an account of politics as an autonomous realm of experience with its own distinct goods, and in order to provide this he has to further refine the mode of practical experience. But can he do this in a non-arbitrary way? Philosophy, as he conceives it, will not deliver this because of the neo-Oakeshottian conception of what a possible political philosophy is, namely, a second-order reflection on things political. This does not identify the concept of the political at all but merely presupposes it, a fact Newey seems to acknowledge when he concedes that there may not be any distinctively political goods after all.[18] For Newey, the concept of the political can only be derived from experience itself. This is emphasized by Newey's Dunn-like plea that political theory needs to be more descriptive and sensitive to political forms as they are actually found in the world, and to conceptions of agency that are more sensitive to the complexity of actual politics.

Appealing to experience is all well and good, but we can approach experience in a variety of ways: for example, we can look at what goes on (the analysis of political behaviour or comparative politics), or reflect on longer patterns of human experience through history. Furthermore, we can look at the way experience has been reflected in thought, the variety of which is given in the history of political thinking. From this multiplicity of political experience, it is assumed we can derive something like Newey's thin but non-arbitrary definition of politics. But is this what we get when we reflect on human experience? There is no obvious reason why we should view politics in this Schmttian, violent 'friend–enemy' way. While this might well reflect part of human experience, it does not necessarily reflect all of human experience. Why, therefore, should this be seen as definitive and not marginal? But let us assume for argument that Newey's thin definition of politics is not arbitrary. Does it necessarily only lead towards the more conflictual Schmittian conception of politics as ceaseless violent struggle? And, more importantly, does it lead to a conception of politics that is autonomous from other things such as ethics and morality?

There were three main components to Newey's view of politics: first, that it consists of endemic disagreement about what counts as politics; second, that there is endemic disagreement among the things that count as politics; and, finally, politics is about power. This conception is supposed to reflect the experience of politics in the real world, therefore it cannot stipulatively exclude politically inconvenient facts. Does this conception of politics ground an exclusively autonomous conception of the political and, therefore, rule political liberalism as being anti-political?

The first feature of politics, namely endemic conflict about what counts as politics, would seem to weaken Newey's argument immediately. The very concept of politics allows endemic disagreement about whether it is or is not a distinct and autonomous mode of experience or sphere of practice. If politics is what it is and not another thing, and people have construed it in as many and as conflicting ways as they have (even looking at only the western tradition of political thinking), then it is hard to see how we can support a non-arbitrary conception of the autonomy of the political. Why does Machiavelli represent the experience of politics any more than Kant, or, more importantly, Locke, Madison and Montesquieu, all of whom were aware of the darker side of politics, the realm of passion, unreason, force and power, as well as the brighter side of reason, agreement and the good life? Newey's Machiavellian approach to politics, with its celebration of contingency and manipulation of power, is just as arbitrary as any narrowly Kantian view. Certainly, it is a good idea for political theorists not to become too one-sided and enamoured of the possibilities of reason, but is it not equally a good idea to avoid becoming too nihilistic and

Machiavellian? While Schmitt gives us the friend–enemy distinction he also gives us a pretty poor account of political judgement.

Where does this leave the claims of liberal political theory? The idea of endemic disagreement about the nature of politics does not preclude the normative vision of political liberalism. All it does is preclude that vision being elevated into an exclusive account of the political. As long as liberal political theory does not attempt to preclude all else in its account of building just political institutions then it is perfectly compatible with the first of Newey's conditions. Does political liberalism need to claim that it exhausts the scope of political theory? No – it merely needs to defend the priority of its approach as an important corrective to the contingencies of political power. Indeed, if we look at normative liberal political theory in the tradition of a limited constitutional politics, we do see precisely the awareness of the problems of political power, which Newey thinks are the peculiar concern of Machiavellian views of politics. It is precisely because of the need to constrain power, and to channel its use in more benign directions, that we have political liberalism's focus on the basic institutional structure of society as opposed to moral paternalism. Constitutionalism and institution-building is an important response to the endemic nature of conflict and power as Newey defines it. That Rawls, Barry and Dworkin do not spend more time discussing this aspect of politics does not mean that their approach is any less political in the relevant sense. What we need, in order to undermine the claims of political liberalism, is an argument that shows it is unable to deliver institutional and constitutional design. Newey thinks that this argument can be built out of the second feature of his account of politics: namely, the fact of endemic disagreement about the things we agree are political.

This second feature of politics ties Newey's argument to those of sceptical pluralists such as Gray and Mouffe. It is supposed to show that liberals assume endemic pluralism in order to ground their impartialist approach to politics, but, because of that, cannot provide an adequate foundation for their political project. The fact of pluralism undercuts the possibility of reasonable consensus and therefore liberal political theory. This issue is a familiar redescription of the standard argument against various liberal theories, claiming they have inadequate theoretical foundations and rest on a conception of false neutrality. (We will examine this criticism directly in the next chapter.) These critiques may or may not prove to be conclusive refutations of particular liberal political theories, but do they preclude their counting as political theories? This argument only works if the character of politics is such as to make the whole liberal enterprise impossible. And it is not proved simply because a particular variant of political liberalism has an inadequate defence of neutrality or impartiality. All then turns on the idea that disagreement is endemic even within the scope of those things identified as political. But is this the case? Again this characterization has to be a generalization of political experience and not a definitional truth. Is it then true that disagreement is endemic even over ends that are agreed to be political? Even if we concede this, it is not obvious that it precludes quite what Newey thinks it precludes. Indeed, even Gray is now inclined to think that it does not preclude all that Newey thinks, for Gray does allow for the possibility of a Hobbesian agreement or modus vivendi. We could construe this second constraint from Newey's argument in a number of ways. If we assume that it rules out any kind of agreement motive, or motive to cooperation, then we are loading a lot into the constraint that is not necessarily borne out by experience. The aspiration to seek fair terms of cooperation might be overridden in many cases and might not have quite the practical priority in ordinary deliberation as it does in the ideal world of liberal political theory, but as long as it remains a possibility and has some motivational force we cannot assume that endemic disagreement precludes the possibility of any agreement. The condition does not rule out the possibility of agreement, but it does caution us about its scope. Any theory that assumes uncontroversially that the moral motive (whatever that is) will always be given practical priority will appear unrealistic. But there are not many such theories. All liberal theories need to do is to be aware of the practical constraints of ideal reasoning, and to have accounts of motivation that are not so ideally demanding that they are precluded by all available evidence. Liberal theories tend to offer pretty thin accounts of motivation that, although not directly derived from our best understanding of social and individual psychology, do not ignore the constraints they impose. Indeed, in the circumstances, the idea that disagreement is as endemic as Newey suggests is counter-intuitive, in that it tends towards a Hobbesian view of the world. Hobbes is often a good guide in politics, but that does not mean his account of human psychology and motivation is necessarily true. If our philosophy is to be as sensitive to experience as Newey thinks a proper political philosophy should be, we also need to be sensitive to the fact that the world, while bleak, is not anything like a Hobbesian state of nature. If we, like Schmitt and Hobbes, build our picture of the world or ordinary politics as a world of war and conflict then we radically distort human experience. Schmitt might well have thought that modernity made the centrality of war and struggle to politics an ever more present reality, but that judgement must be contextualized. If politics is war by other means then it is no longer really war, and we should focus on the intricacies of why it is not. Disagreement is as central to civility as it is to war and struggle. Disagreement is as much a feature of scholarship as it is of a Machiavellian vision of politics. That does not mean that either no agreement is ever possible, or that disagreement is always violent and conflictual. Thus disagreement may be endemic, but we do not have to assume without further evidence that disagreement about everything is endemic. That has not been shown and does not strictly follow from Newey's second condition.

If on the other hand his point is that the priority of reason is required to carry too much in liberal theory, and that this ignores the ineliminability of other non-rational motives, then he again provides a useful corrective to a potential narrowness in liberal theory, but he does not preclude it. Indeed, if we look at thinkers who have seen institutional design and constitutionalism as ways of binding agents to goods they really want but often act against, then we can see how a political theory could acknowledge the variety of human motivation without being unduly rationalistic or collapsing back into a celebration of contingency, force and passion. Passion is certainly a force in politics, but it is no more sensible to elevate passion to an unassailable first principle than it is to elevate reason. The world is more complex than Newey suggests, and liberals are not required to deny that fact.

Finally, politics is characterized by power. As will have been clear from what I have said about the other two conditions, there is no good reason to assume that the preoccupation with the manipulation of power takes us any closer to a Machiavellian view of politics than a Lockean or Madisonian view. Certainly, it is helpful to correct the liberal preoccupation with constitutional politics by a recognition of its other manifestations. But there is nothing in liberal political theory to warrant the claim that the construction of a just basic structure equals the end of history. Again we are offered a reason to broaden the scope of liberal political theory, not a reason to deny that it is political at all. Indeed, the Schmittian elevation of politics to violent struggle between friend and enemy is only a fetish, and one we should rightly be wary of.

Given that the account of politics that Newey operates with does not support the idea of a set of distinctively political goods that excludes those moral goods pursued by liberal theory, the two main strands of his critique are inconclusive. The reduction of politics to ethics is not necessarily a reduction at all, but merely an acknowledgement that politics is either a branch of ethics, as Aristotle thought, or that one is not identical with the other, although they are connected. This seems to be the position of most prominent liberal theorists. If reductivism fails then the force of the instrumentalist critique is also undercut. After all, at a sufficient level of generality one could argue that Aristotle has an instrumental view of politics. Instrumentalism is a problem only if there are peculiarly political goods that are categorically distinct from ethical goods, broadly conceived. If there are such goods, Newey has not identified them, and neither has he provided an adequate account of why we should see politics as a categorically distinct realm of experience.

In the end we do not have to choose simply between Machiavelli and the celebration of contingency, struggle and manipulation, or Kant and the eradication of contingency. It is only the tyranny of inadequate theory that makes our choices so black and white. As with most things the correct view is somewhere in the middle, a middle that is occupied by Locke, Montesquieu, Madison, Mill and much contemporary political liberalism, as set out in previous chapters. These thinkers are not concerned with eradicating contingency, but equally they do not concede all to chance and struggle (indeed, neither did Machiavelli). Instead, they see political theory as an attempt to build dykes and channels for human action, in the hope of directing it towards better goals and reinforcing human purposes that would otherwise be difficult to sustain. This is not utopian, unrealistic or the denial of politics, but is merely one further manifestation of how humans do politics. If political liberalism is to fail it has to do so for a more substantial set of reasons. In the next chapter we will look at whether political liberalism is ethnocentric and, therefore, of only local interest to western liberal democracies.

7
False Neutrality and Ethnocentrism

Having argued that political liberalism can indeed count as a political theory that does not distort or ignore the realities of politics, I have addressed one of the major challenges to it. While important, that still leaves open the far more important question of whether political liberalism is adequate on other grounds, and, most importantly, whether its philosophical foundations are sufficiently robust to support its political ambitions. Not least of these is whether political liberalism can provide citizens with reasons for acting or forbearing from acting in certain ways, and provide states with reasons for restricting the exercise of coercive power. Both of these points go to the heart of the practical significance of political liberalism.

The issue of the foundations of political liberalism opens deep philosophical questions that cannot be fully answered in a book such as this, as they go to the heart of the nature and scope of political philosophy. While I cannot develop a direct and comprehensive defence of political liberalism, I want to contribute to an indirect defence of political liberalism by arguing that some of the standard challenges to political liberalism are less devastating than they are claimed to be. In particular, I want to address two questions that have dominated much contemporary discussion of political liberalism: namely, whether it is ethnocentric, and whether it rests on a false conception of neutrality. The latter charge is levelled by thinkers who are often grouped under the heading of communitarianism,[1] and the former charge is levelled by multiculturalist thinkers.[2] Not all communitarians are multiculturalists and not all multiculturalists are communitarians. Nevertheless, both positions share a common concern that political liberalism imposes its own local and partial morality as a universal perspective, in order to arbitrate impartially between the claims of groups and cultures. Both positions challenge what they take to be the bogus universalism of liberalism. Taken together, these two positions present the main opposition to liberalism. As with the argument of the previous chapter, by showing that these critiques are inadequate, I will not have provided an alternative independent justification of political liberalism. That said, by challenging these criticisms, this chapter will provide additional support for taking seriously the project of seeking foundations for political liberalism, by showing that the project is not misconceived.

Before turning to the substance of the ethnocentric and false neutrality challenges, I need to say something in general about what is at issue concerning the foundations of liberalism. In chapter 3 we saw how political liberalism has tended to deploy the idea of a reasonable agreement as the basis for its claim to provide authoritative reasons for distributing rights, liberties and resources. Reasonable agreement develops from the idea of a hypothetical contract that has its roots in the social contract tradition going back through Kant and Rousseau to Locke and Hobbes. A principle distributing basic liberties is, therefore, justified in so far as it could be accepted, or not reasonably rejected, as the basis for a fair scheme of social cooperation by anyone to whom it applies. Against the requirement of reasonable agreement, critics often refer to the fact of reasonable disagreement as an endemic feature of modern societies, and the absence of agreement on liberal principles as a problem for political liberalism with its claims to provide binding and authoritative reasons. This was indeed one of the arguments we saw rehearsed in the previous chapter.

However, the fact of disagreement or the absence of agreement proves nothing: it is merely a restatement of one of the circumstances within which the search for reasonable agreement becomes important. The reason it proves nothing in itself is that it is a fact, and as such needs to be explained. One possible explanation is that the fact of disagreement reveals the limitations of reason and the impossibility of establishing reasonable agreement between people who adhere to rival moral schemes and traditions. This argument is used to underpin many of the communitarian and multiculturalist criticisms of liberalism, but it is only one possible explanation. There are many other reasons why people disagree about the terms of political association, some of which can explain its absence but do not rule out its possibility. The issue for us must be the philosophical one about the possibility of reasonable agreement, as it is this alone which would rule out liberalism. While sociological, historical, political and psychological explanations of the absence of agreement are not unimportant, they do not settle the issue of the viability of political liberalism. These factors might well show that it is difficult to transfer liberal values that have a particular historical origin into another political culture, but they do not show that it is either impossible or wrong to do so.

Ethnocentrism and false neutrality

Chapter 3 shows how liberalism develops from the contract tradition in conceiving of the state as a fair system of social cooperation shaped by a series of principles that ensure the equal treatment of all people. This commitment to fundamental equal treatment requires the state to be impartial in matters of fundamental moral significance and disagreement. This political impartialism is what makes political liberalism *liberal* as opposed to *paternalist*. However, as I suggested in that chapter, following Barry, this commitment to impartiality should be seen as a second-order commitment applying to the basic structure of society and not as a first-order decision rule to be applied in ordinary practical deliberation.

That said, many contemporary critics of liberalism have objected to this more modest conception of impartiality on the grounds that it still embodies the partial perspective of a particular liberal morality. Instead of providing an impartial language for dealing with disputes between rival moral claims, liberalism is merely another contestable moral position. If liberalism is merely the prejudice of a particular society or culture, it cannot provide reasons that apply beyond its own boundaries and, therefore, it fails to be universal. The whole aspiration of the contract tradition to justify an impartialist political framework is a chimera. Versions of this argument can be found in a number of communitarian thinkers, such as Michael Sandel and Alasdair MacIntyre, but most recently it has been taken up by multiculturalist critics of liberalism, such as Bhikhu Parekh, James Tully and Iris Marion Young. These multiculturalists are most interesting from the perspective of this argument because they combine an assault on the idea of the false neutrality and ethnocentrism of liberal universalism, with an assertion of political pluralism and a challenge to the idea of state sovereignty. The privilege political liberalism attaches to state sovereignty derives from the idea of a single ultimate and unified site of political authority that is the source of exceptionless general laws. As liberal universalism is seen to deny pluralism and difference, so the idea of sovereignty is seen as a denial of the authority of forms of association such as cultures, minority national groupings, or forms of association that acknowledge authority beyond the state, such as many religions. We will return to this issue in the next chapter. In this chapter we will focus on the critique of universalism and impartiality offered by these communitarian and multiculturalist critics.

The problem with impartiality for these critics is that it assumes that it is possible to adopt an impartialist perspective that is neutral between rival conceptions of the good life or political values. Yet impartialist theories always endorse the priority of core liberal values such as that accorded to the individual, the value of equality of concern and respect, or freedom of expression. Multiculturalists argue that liberal political rights always prevail because the whole system is premised on the idea of persons as free and equal moral agents, precisely the claim that is advanced earlier in this book. The problem is that these values are contested and some groups within liberal societies claim these are not impartial values, but merely a reflection of the dominant culture of liberal democratic states. Hence minority cultural groups with practices that afford subordinate status to women will always find themselves disadvantaged in a liberal state. Multiculturalist critics of impartiality thus claim that liberals do not guarantee genuine equality of concern and respect because they do not afford equality of recognition to all identity-conferring associations, but only to those that are already substantively liberal. This is not because of the super-iority of liberal values, but is merely a reflection of the fact that liberal individualism is the dominant political culture in liberal democratic states. Other people, who are not part of this dominant liberal culture, usually immigrants or aborigi-nal 'first nations', will end up bearing the burdens of costly beliefs and practices simply because of this dominance of liberalism. The liberal theorist might well concede that the implications of an impartial constitution do have the effect of rendering certain choices and beliefs more burdensome than others, and yet respond that this is not a relevant criti-cism because the impartialist perspective sets the framework of legitimation within which individuals or groups can pursue their own ends. After all, no one has a right to find their beliefs and choices unburdensome and some who choose to commit criminal or civil wrongs will find their beliefs and choices very costly indeed. The problem with this liberal response is that it only succeeds if liberals can show that the impartialist perspective is not merely a further local concep-tion of political values. If liberal values are merely the local prejudices of the European Enlightenment, then they are not universal and cannot have any claim on people who do not share these European values. This is the *enthocentric* objection. Liberal values are not universal and, therefore, a basis for impartial reconciliation of conflicting moral claims and systems. Rather, liberal values are merely the values of a particular European culture with a particular history. They are our values, if we are Europeans or descendants of a Euro-pean culture such as the United States, but that is their only authority. If we are not already liberals, as might be the case with non-European immigrants or first nations in previously colonized states, then it is not obvious that failure to attach priority to liberal values is acting unreasonably. If it cannot be shown that liberal values are more than simply the local values of western democracies, then they are merely the ethnocentric prejudices of a particular society and have no authority beyond the boundaries of that society. Thus it is liberalism for the liberals and cannibalism for the cannibals.[3]

Multiculturalist critics reinforce this charge of the ethnocentrism of political liberalism by providing historicized accounts of the theories or arguments used to support it. James Tully, for example, argues that liberal constitutionalism is merely a cultural phenomenon from late-modern Europe, and as such has no obvious authority over the claims made for, and by, indigenous aboriginal peoples. The extension of liberal constitutionalism to some post-communist or non-European nations is merely a form of cultural imperialism.[4] That such constitutional forms might be desirable outside of the cultures within which they originated is certainly possible, but this is a matter of political contingency and not of the supposed universal applicability of these arguments. It is not the case, according to Tully, that any non-western state that chose not to adopt a fully liberal or impartial constitution would be failing in rationality.[5]

In light of this relativist anti-universalism, multiculturalist critics such as Parekh, Tully and Young argue that the appropriate terms of association and integration of groups in society must be settled by political means and not by some supposed pre-political philosophical argument of liberal theory. Given that such a strategy does not simply result in secession and fragmentation, the expectation of such theorists is that the terms of cooperation and integration would allow considerable group autonomy, and discretion for each group to regulate its own affairs on the model of state sovereignty. Instead of a model of individuals contracting to create fair terms of social cooperation, we have a model of cultural groups and interests contracting, but in the absence of any pre-existing norm of fairness that would overcome the facts of positional advantage and unequal bargaining power.[6]

For such theories, impartiality is not merely a myth, but is a pernicious myth because it masks the exercise of coercive power by political majorities or dominant political interests under the guise of principle and justice. We have dominance masquerading as justice and fairness. This is the charge that has been advanced by multiculturalists and advocates of group rights, and by pluralist anti-liberals such as John Gray.[7] The question remains whether such charges actually stick.

The key premise of the anti-liberal's argument is that the basic norm of reasonableness that underlies its account of consent and legitimacy is always particular and local, rather than universal and impartial. It is always some group's conception of reason, and therefore reflects the particular interests and values of that group. Reason is never reason as such, but always *western* reason, reflecting the 'prejudices' of the European Enlightenment project.[8] This premise depends on seeing reason as merely a relational concept linking actions to desires, or beliefs to evidence. Reason is also seen as substantively loaded, and inextricable from moral ends or values. On this understanding reason cannot be distinguished from the context in which a statement or proposition becomes a reason for some particular end. Alasdair MacIntyre, for example, claims that the liberal's use of reason divorces it from this teleological structure, where reasonableness always depends on an account of the end (*telos*) being pursued.[9] If reasonableness is a substantive concept as MacIntyre and other communitarians claim, then it will not be possible to divorce the concept from the conceptual schemes or cultural practices that give rise to accounts of these ends. By situating the concept of reason within distinct conceptual schemes or cultural practices, the liberal cannot be genuinely neutral between different conceptions of the good life or political value. Yet if the liberal concedes this and simply asserts the superiority of his own conceptual scheme above others, then he concedes the relativist conclusion of the ethnocentric and multiculturalist objection. It really is liberalism for the liberals and cannibalism for the cannibals! More pressingly, it also means that in multicultural societies there is no possibility of impartial reasons for arbitrating between the claims of rival groups. Instead, such pressing issues will be left to the vagaries of political compromise, in which the most powerful group will always be able to dictate the terms. Within the state, and beyond it in the international realm, there is simply the rule of force.

The possibility of universalism

If liberalism is merely a local cultural prejudice then much if not all of its authority quickly evaporates. The key question we must address is whether the charge of ethnocentrism and false neutrality is as devastating as claimed. In this section I want to provide indirect support for the universalist character of political liberalism by challenging the basis of the anti-universalist case. The ethnocentric and anti-neutralist case distinguishes between the capacity to reason, which is generic and universal, and reasons, which are not. Moral and political reasons, it is claimed, are always situated, contextualized and parochial. But why should liberals concede this point? Why should they accept that the reasons used to support political liberalism are merely reasons for liberals and not for anyone else?

The argument against universalism involves a number of distinct moves. First, it argues, as we have seen, that reasons are always internal to some conceptual scheme or culture. Second, it claims that beyond such a scheme they are reasonably contestable, and, finally, it points to the huge variety of different conceptual schemes, cultures or conceptions of the good – by which we mean comprehensive moral doctrines. In contrast to this view, the universalist is supposed to be committed to the idea of universal reason as the view from nowhere – one which does not presuppose any controversial or disputed moral notion. Unless this view is upheld the idea of neutrality is a fraud, as it will always involve drawing on controversial beliefs. Glen Newey advances a version of this argument against contractualists such as Rawls, Barry and Scanlon.[10]

In response to Newey's account of liberalism's predicament, the liberal can simply reject the idea of strict neutrality. Political liberalism does not have to avoid drawing on any controversial values at all. Indeed it cannot avoid them, as it draws on at least the idea of equality of concern and respect, thus putting it at odds with fundamentally inegalitarian views. This is precisely the strategy of Barry, who claims to be an impartialist and not a neutralist; it is also the strategy of Rawls, who concedes that his theory of justice draws on a thin theory of the good. The question is whether this rejection of strict neutralism is a concession too far, as Newey suggests. What might make it so is the claim that all reasons are narrowly context-dependent, and therefore that any belief that is controversial elsewhere must necessarily fail to count as a universal reason. Thus, if some group somewhere rejects fundamental equality in favour of a caste-based account of inequality, then liberalism's egalitarian premise cannot serve as a universal basis for liberal principles. But, as we have seen, the fact of rejection does not prove that a reason is not a reason; rejection itself has to be reasonable and not simply based on the protection of a group interest or a sectional advantage. As we are concerned with reasonable rejection, we come back to the issue of whether reasons are narrowly contextualized and local. Why should we accept this view?

Perhaps the strongest reason for thinking that reasons are always contextualized and local is derived from what is called the fact of pluralism. This is simply the view that there are a wide variety of beliefs, perspectives and cultures, all of which differ in important respects. Sociologists, anthropologists and historians remind us of the manifold diversity of human experience. Difference, diversity and pluralism seem to be the norm of human life, not sameness, or universality. We should expect to see a variety of ways of doing things, including organizing political communities. Each of these varied ways of doing things is a response to the particularities of human experience. Consequently, we should not expect to find commonality, nor, more importantly, should we expect to find a single or universal right way of organizing human affairs. As liberals are committed to the idea of a single right way of organizing human affairs, they run up against the fact of pluralism.[11]

Whilst the fact of difference and pluralism does pose a challenge to liberalism, it remains unclear what precisely that challenge is and how seriously we should take it. After all, the liberal aspiration is to provide a framework within which difference can be channelled in benign and non-conflictual directions, so in that sense it is an accommodation to, and not a denial of, difference. The idea that political liberalism aspires to impose a uniformity on ways of living is a misapprehension. It does not propose uniformity of outcomes but merely uniform general laws that apply to all in the regulation of social interaction, where the content of those laws reflects equal basic rights and liberties. As liberalism is not concerned with denying difference as such, the assertion of the fact of pluralism is neither here nor there. The denial of universalism must, therefore, be based on something more than the fact of pluralism. The key point seems to be that the fact of pluralism shows that there is only diversity, and there is no impartial space within which to construct a set of universal reasons for regulating diversity. Once again, liberalism must simply be the expression of the partiality of liberals. However, suppose liberalism's universal reasons are not simply plucked from a realm beyond context – they are not a priori, as philosophers like to express it – but instead are constructed from reasons, beliefs and values that are situated in social and historical contexts, yet have a reach or scope that goes beyond those contexts. In so far as they have this scope, their truth or validity is not context-dependent in the relevant sense and thus the enthnocentric objection can be ignored. That this is not such a counter-intuitive idea can be shown through the universal scope of theoretical reason. No one seriously claims that because Euclidean geometry developed in a particular historical culture its truth claims are constrained to the boundaries of the ancient Greek *polis*. Nor does anyone seriously assert that some of the key concepts of modern arithmetic hold only in the Sanskrit culture of ancient India or in the Arabic world, because they first appeared in these particular historical contexts. Of course one can argue that, although not culturally particular, these theoretical concepts are still particular to a conceptual scheme, as modern mathematicians have developed non-Euclidean geometries that challenge the idea that Euclidean Geometry provides a true final description of the properties of objects in space. But, if the critique of universalism depends on the possibility of showing that conceptual schemes are discrete and translation between them is impossible, then the critique itself arguably rests on a philosophical position that is either non-proven or problematic.[12] To show that the idea of distinct conceptual schemes makes sense, one would need to show that there are concepts or beliefs in one scheme that cannot be translated into another scheme. But, as Donald Davidson argues, this is a deeply paradoxical claim as it presupposes that we can identify the difference and irreducibility between the two concepts, which does seem to suggest that we can translate and therefore understand the same concepts. If we can understand across conceptual schemes then we have a problem in identifying their boundaries, or what it is that distinguishes one scheme from another. The best analogy we have for what seems to underlie the idea of a distinct conceptual scheme is the idea of a natural language. Chinese is different from English in that different words are used; the question remains whether translation is possible between the two. It would seem that complex concepts from one language can be translated into the other, just as complex systems of thought like Confucianism can be translated into English. For example nineteenth-century Chinese translators, such as Yen Fu, were able to translate English liberals, such as J. S. Mill and Herbert Spencer, into Chinese.[13] The counter-claim is that something is lost in translation and that certain important nuances are often obscured. Yet this takes us back to the original point that, in order to be able to state or describe what is lost, we need to be able to obtain a high degree of translatability across natural languages. The same must also be true of conceptual schemes unless these can be given a determinate structure that is different from natural languages. We can make similar arguments against multiculturalist theorists, who offer 'culture' as an alternative closed or clearly bounded belief system that precludes the idea of universal reasons and values. The idea of culture has become very fashionable among political theorists as a way of defending difference against the supposed homogenizing tendencies of universalist liberalism. But, just as philosophers of language have raised questions about the coherence of referring to discrete conceptual schemes, so anthropologists (whose academic discipline was supposed to be the study of culture) have turned a more sceptical eye on the concept. Consequently, even political theorists who are sensitive to claims of difference and pluralism accuse much of the use of culture in political theory of resting on a 'poor man's sociology'.[14] Other anthropologists have been much more critical of culture as a useful explanatory concept. Therefore it almost seems as if political theorists have taken on a largely discredited concept just as its original disciplinary host has become more and more uncomfortable with it.[15] Before I appear to collapse into a reactionary stance, let me just clarify the point being made about culture. I am not denying the significance that people attach to familiar beliefs and practices, or the general need to show sensitivity to those practices in liberal legislation. In so far as that is the multiculturalist claim, it is uncontroversial for liberals (and I would claim that many multiculturalist theorists are liberals as we are using the term). What I am denying is the stronger claim, often also advanced by multiculturalist critics, to the effect that cultures themselves serve as discrete conceptual schemes that preclude the possibility of universalist norms and principles.[16] The conception of culture that would be necessary to preclude universalism and support the ethnocentric objection remains incoherent and unsupported in contemporary anthropology. Furthermore, I am rejecting what Benhabib has described as the 'poor man's sociology' view of culture, which asserts that cultures are fixed and stable over time, so that any reprioritizing of beliefs and practices would involve the radical destruction of a culture. Frequently this view is offered as an explanation of why the extension of some internal norms or privileges within one culture, such as equalizing opportunities for women, cannot be made without doing irreparable damage to the culture's identity. It is in fact an argument for a version of conservatism, and one that is particularly attractive to those on the far right of the political spectrum.

In the end, the idea of conceptual relativism that underlies the ethnocentric objection is notoriously difficult to state, let alone defend. Thus there is no obvious reason why value concepts and sets of beliefs that emerge in one place and time cannot be accepted as authoritative or action-guiding beyond that historical context. Of course, this does not show that the particular value concepts and beliefs that underpin liberalism have a universal scope, but equally it does undermine the claims of culturalists and particularists that universal reasons are not possible. What it does allow is that the claim of liberalism to draw on universal reasons does not fall at the first hurdle, as is often argued.

Having dispensed with the ethnocentric objection as a serious obstacle to liberal aspirations to universality, I still need to clarify the form of universalism that is given indirect support. What I have not defended is the idea of an abstract meta-language into which all values can be translated and weighed against each other. Liberalism is often accused of using precisely this conception of the universality of reason due to its use of concepts such as utility, as a common medium into which all other values can be translated and then compared and prioritized. This is certainly the aspiration behind utilitarianism, where utility is used as the medium for measuring all first-order values such as liberty, equality, security, community or individuality. Many liberals have been utilitarians and at least two of the founders of modern utilitarianism, Jeremy Bentham and John Stuart Mill, have been liberals. Not all contemporary utilitarians would identify themselves as liberals. Communitarian critics of liberalism, such as MacIntyre, and multiculturalist theorists, such as Parekh, accuse liberalism of deploying this kind of external meta-language approach to universalism. This interpretation of liberal universalism has also been used to underpin criticisms of liberalism based on the incommensurability of values or beliefs, a view that has been deployed most forcefully by John Gray, but which is also associated with Joseph Raz and ultimately Isaiah Berlin.[17] Incommensurability theorists such as Gray attempt to resurrect a version of the ethnocentric objection by arguing that the moral practices of different societies are incommensurable, or not reducible to a higher-order meta-language, such as utility or welfare. The consequence of incommensurability, so understood, is that it undercuts the possibility of making universal claims about the cardinal ranking of distinct values such as liberty. The rankings of different values and principles will be internal to cultures or moral practices and there is no external perspective from which one can argue that one ranking is superior to another. Thus, it is argued, we cannot say that one set of moral practices that secures gender equality is superior to another set that asserts inequality and patriarchy.

The incommensurability thesis is supposed to overthrow the possibility of liberal universalism, but does it? Two things can be said at the outset which limit the scope of the incommensurability thesis. The first is that it is not the case that political liberalism does require the idea of full commensurability between moral practices and systems. The universalist case focuses on discrete values and principles, and not systems of value and belief, where the challenge might well be more plausible. The incommensurability thesis needs to show that moral practices and systems have to be judged all of a piece and not as discrete components. Liberalism in its political variant, as discussed in this book, does not offer a comprehensive moral scheme, but rather a set of commitments that guarantee equality of concern and respect in terms of the distribution of basic rights, protections and resources. Second, the thesis assumes that liberalism must deploy an external meta-language into which the rival claims of values and norms that are internal to moral systems and practices can be judged. Once again, we can raise questions about whether moral and political practices are discrete and therefore incommensurable. Certainly it is the case that different groups of people do different things, but once again we have to be careful about the moral we draw from that. But, leaving that issue to one side, does political liberalism need to appeal to an external meta-language such as utility or welfare? At one level the answer is clearly no. Although utilitarians have to concede this charge, it does not mean that all liberals must. There are numerous non-utilitarian liberalisms, and, as I suggested earlier, the most profitable understanding of political liberalism is as a non-utilitarian doctrine. Incommensurability, where it obtains, rules out the possibility of a cardinal ranking of alternatives, but unless that is exactly what liberals need in order to support rational arguments about values and principles, then it is not a decisive objection to the possibility of reasoned argument about values. If the incommensurability thesis is weakened, so that it merely claims that there is no non-particularistic perspective from which we can decide what are the best principles for ordering political society, then it collapses back into a version of the ethnocentric objection that we dispensed with earlier. It is this sense of the thesis that is deployed by Gray and others, yet it is the stronger version of the thesis that carries whatever intuitive plausibility the incommensurability thesis has. While that version may well prove problematic for utilitarians, the problem does not extend to all forms of liberalism. Crucially, it does not affect the conception of political liberalism we are deploying, as that does not seek to commensurate the various values of different societies into an external language, such as utility or welfare, despite what communitarian critics of liberalism claim.

What is clear, throughout the discussion so far, is that the criticisms of liberal universalism derive much of their plausibility from the distinction between moral principles and values as *internal* to cultures, conceptual schemes and societies, or else as *external* to these things. Moral principles have to be either internal or external. This is precisely the dichotomy used by communitarians such as MacIntyre, Taylor and Walzer.[18] It is also a distinction that many liberals are often accused of falling victim to, including Rawls in *Political Liberalism*. Rawls' appeal to the idea of an overlapping consensus between reasonable comprehensive doctrines, which he uses to justify his account of justice as fairness without appealing to a liberal conception of the good, appears to be yet another version of the ethnocentric objection. Rawls introduces the idea of reasonable comprehensive doctrines in his later work, as integreted systems of moral beliefs and practices. This, according to Brian Barry, is merely a concession to the internalist view, exemplified most clearly by the communitarian theorist Michael Walzer. Rawls' aim is to provide a justification of justice as fairness by showing how it could be said to rest on the consent of a series of 'reasonable' comprehensive moral views. The crucial point here is the idea of consent; each comprehensive view endorses the free-standing idea of justice as fairness from within its own moral framework. Although this does not commit Rawls to appeal to an external standard independent and prior to this convergence of comprehensive doctrines, it does rest on the idea that liberalism's principles are universal only in so far as they are the result of a convergence or overlap of internalist perspectives. This view makes the whole enterprise of Rawls' account of justice as fairness contingent on the idea of endorsement from within the comprehensive moral doctrines of those discussing justice or fair terms of social cooperation, but abandons the idea of the claim of reason as an independent ground for endorsement. But the whole point about the prior authority of comprehensive moral doctrines again depends upon the limited scope of reason, which is central to the internalist view. While there are many liberal reasons for tolerating the widest pluralism of comprehensive moral doctrines, consistent with equal concern and respect of each person, the argument for this should not rest on the limited scope of reason. This is a concession too far, and one that potentially weakens the value of Rawls' profound contribution to liberalism in *A Theory of Justice*. [19]

Yet, if the liberal rejects the idea of situated or ethnocentric reason, then she must accept the idea of an *external* view, precisely the precarious metaphysical position Rawls was trying to avoid. The critics of externalism try to support the internalist perspective by questioning what this *external* view amounts to. Does it for example depend on an ideal meta-language, such as utility, that leads to the challenge from incommensurability? This is the version of the claim employed by sceptical liberals such as John Gray.

Despite this attempt to queer the idea of externalism, the point of my defence of liberal universalism against the ethnocentric objection has not been to assert its truth but to dispense with the distinction altogether. It is a central claim of liberal universalism that its reasons are reasons as such, not the reasons of particular groups, historical communities or localities. It is precisely this view that underpins Barry's (apparently dismissive) view of the authority of culture as simply reducing to the claim 'this is how we do things around here'. The point, though polemical, is precisely to challenge the automatic authority of culture or received beliefs. Appeal to cultural beliefs and practices is not an argument, unless some version of the ethnocentric argument it true. By challenging the possibility of an uncontroversial statement of the internal/external distinction, liberalism can at least claim that the idea of reasons that are universal in scope is not an incoherent or question-begging notion. Of course, this still leaves open the need to identify those reasons and to build an adequate justification of liberal principles. I cannot provide such a defence here, although clearly my preferred approach would be some variant of the contractarian arguments discussed in chapter 3. Yet the criticisms of the ethnocentric objection in this chapter are not insignificant, as most standard criticisms of universalism appeal to the idea of culture and conceptual schemes as if they were unproblematic notions, and as if they had fixed contents and clear bound-aries. Without the ethnocentric objection it is unclear what precisely is wrong with liberalism's claim to universality.

However, before this is seen as an endorsement of liberal triumphalism that allows for the imperialistic extension of liberal culture across the globe, we need to remind ourselves of precisely what is being defended here. The liberal does not deny diversity and difference, nor the existence of different institutional practices. It is simply a red herring to assert that the defence of liberal universalism will tend towards same-ness. The possibility of the reasonable justification of liberal-ism still leaves considerable work for liberals to do. It should also be pointed out that political liberals, while endorsing the idea of the universality of scope of reasons, also recognize the limits of reason in reducing all disagreement. To reiterate what was said at the end of the last chapter, liberals aspire to justify principles and rights that channel difference and reasonable disagreement. What liberals reject is both the idea that reason can justify the imposition of a single uniform way of living for all men, and the opposite idea, namely that all disagreement is reasonable and that there is no possibility of setting boundaries around acceptable and non-acceptable forms of social and political association.

Why seek agreement?

There remains one very complex issue that I have not addressed in giving my defence of the possibility of liberal universalism, and this is the philosophically vexed question: why does reason motivate? Why is it that because I have a reason to seek fair terms of social cooperation I should be motivated to treat others with equality of concern and respect in various ways? It is primarily because of this normative or action-guiding aspect of moral or political reasons that practical reasonableness is not thought to be the same as theoretical reason. Nothing much follows (practically) from theoretical reasons about the nature of triangles unless we have some independent reason to make this matter – for example, if we are engineers, school teachers or pupils wanting to pass exams. There is no special 'to be doneness' or 'not to be doneness' that follows from theoretical reason. Yet the claim that each person has certain basic rights, or a claim on resources, does have such a normative force. It would be bizarre to claim that one acknowledges that all people should be treated equally as the bearers of rights, and then to continue denying equal treatment and causing suffering to some of them. Practical reasons do claim to have that normative force or action-requiring quality. By what virtue do they have that action-requiring quality? No simple answer can be provided here, or perhaps anywhere else, as the issue of the source of normativity is a generic problem facing all accounts of moral and political principles. In this respect the problem is no more peculiar to liberalism than to any other theory, but it does require some consideration here. The reason for this follows from the dominant philosophical accounts of normativity, or the action-guiding nature of reasons. I will leave out of account crude realist or Thrasymachean (after the character in Plato's *Republic*) accounts, which reduce all moral and political rules to the coercively imposed will of the most powerful. Apart from this pessimistic vision, there are two rival theories: that normativity is based on prudence or the concurrence of a moral belief, value or principle with a pre-existing desire; and that practical reasons have an intrinsic motivational quality that is independent of a concurrent desire. The former view is historically associated with Thomas Hobbes and David Hume, while the latter view is most famously associated with the German philosopher Immanual Kant. Why this matters for the defence of liberal universalism is that the Humean view, of normativity based on desire, is used by parochialists, such as communitarians, to claim the limited scope of moral and political principles because of the limits of sympathy and desire. The claim is that if the scope of our sympathies and desires is naturally limited, then that means the scope of moral and political principles is itself limited. This would be a practical limit to the scope of liberal principles, but a significant limitation all the same. Most importantly, it has the potential implication of allowing the significance of liberalism's core ethical commitment to the equal treatment of persons as such to diminish, the further away people happen to be.

Although this might still allow liberalism in one country, the issue of size would matter in terms of deciding what a viable liberal state would look like. It would limit the global scope of liberal principles, so that there could not be a liberal international law or cosmopolitan order based on liberal principles. If ought implies can, and then it turns out we just cannot as a matter of psychology extend the same concern across great distances, then it might seem that the universal scope of liberal principles collapses. But, again, should we derive a pessimistic anti-universalist implication from this account of psychology? Is the only alternative to retreat to an endorsement of a Kantian-style perspective as the only way of salvaging the idea of normative principles? Many liberals do adopt the view that they cannot avoid recourse to a metaphysics of the self or will, which explains the fact of normativity. Other liberals, especially those within the contractualist tradition such as the early Rawls, Brian Barry and T. M. Scanlon, have tried to avoid addressing the issue of normativity or the motivation to act morally. Barry, following Scanlon, claims that it is the task of a political theory of justice to specify what justice is, and that it can simply rely on a 'motive to act justly' to explain why people would then act justly. The agreement motive, as he describes it, might simply be a natural fact of human psychology illustrated by the desire of many people to act justly, whatever acting justly turns out to involve. Whatever it is, the agreement motive is deliberately under theorized in Barry's *Justice as Impartiality*. The question is, does it matter and does it help address the particularist's rejection of the possibility of universally binding or action-guiding principles?

Why I think it might not matter again turns on the weakness of the particularist's case. By making the case for particularism turn on psychology the particularist is in danger of making the claim highly contingent. Furthermore, it might well be the case that our natural sympathies can be tutored and enlarged. That was actually Hume's view, although he thought the process was limited. In our more globalized world, where we can actually see on our television screens cases of unjust treatment of people beyond the scope of our domestic political communities, perhaps our sympathies and natural reasons for acting justly are universally extendable. All we need to show is that people can extend their moral sympathies beyond their nearest and dearest and beyond the boundaries of their neighbourhood or tribe, and that people can be shown to have a motive to act justly or to seek agreement or social cooperation on fair terms. The question then is to try and specify what those terms are – that is what liberalism claims to provide. The fact that lots of people are concerned with the issue of just terms of social cooperation and treatment, beyond borders, shows that we can act in accordance with universal reasons. The fact that not all do, only shows that normative argument is not merely a description of what groups and individuals actually do, but is rather concerned with why they ought to so act.

The case against liberal universalism is unproven; this does not prove the truth of political liberalism, but it does significantly weaken the force of one of the strongest lines of criticism of liberalism, namely that it is merely one among a plurality of ethnocentric moral practices, no one of which has any more authority than the other.

8
Liberalism, the State and Beyond

In this final chapter I want to turn from the issue of the possibility of moral universalism, and the scope of liberal reasons, to another political implication of the cultural turn in contemporary political theory. This issue concerns the central role of the modern state in contemporary liberalism. Underlying the multiculturalist assault on liberalism are in fact two distinct, though related, issues. The first concerns issues of cultural relativism of the sort we discussed in the previous chapter. But the second set of issues is more directly political and concerns liberalism's commitment to a particular conception of the modern sovereign state. In particular many multiculturalists, such as Iris Marion Young, James Tully and Bhikhu Parekh, are concerned with the way in which the ideal of the sovereign state, inherited from Europe in the sixteenth century, imposes a single uniformity of relations between groups within the state's sphere of influence.[1] That uniformity is imposed from above by a distinct and unitary sovereign body and it is that idea which is central to the modern conception of the juridical state.[2] Contemporary theories of the state offer many more sophisticated accounts of what 'statehood' consists of than those offered by either Thomas Hobbes or Jean Bodin in the sixteenth century, yet the idea of state sovereignty still has a strong pull. This is perhaps most clear in the dominant realist paradigm of international relations theory, which still uses the theme of state sovereignty as its fundamental premise.[3]

The role of the state within liberal theory brings us to the third major strand of critique. Particularists and historicists have been keen to point out that the idea of the sovereign state is a peculiar historical legacy, appropriate to the experience of Europe from the sixteenth to the twentieth century, but by no means one that is universally valid or desirable. As that legacy is placed under critical scrutiny by pluralists and multiculturalists, it loses some of its authority and consequently so does a 'statist' theory such as political liberalism. As radical political theorists of various descriptions seek to think beyond the state, liberalism with its state-centred focus offers at best a narrow conservative stance that is locked into an increasingly redundant political vocabulary. This latter point is taken up most forcefully in the ideas of those cosmopolitan political theorists who work at the interface between state-centred political theory and international relations theory, and who argue for a new vocabulary and set of institutions appropriate to a globalizing world that seems to offer less and less scope for the idea of centralized and unitary sovereign power.

This chapter will examine both challenges to liberalism: its narrow reliance on a unitary conception of sovereignty within its borders, and the challenge to the redundancy of this traditional conception of sovereignty in light of the globalization of economic and political interdependence. This latter challenge will be particularly important, as it has encouraged a new cosmopolitan approach to political theory that builds on some of the ideas about rights and egalitarian social justice at the heart of the liberal perspective we have explored in this book. In conclusion, we will assess the extent to which cosmopolitanism is the future for what I have described as political liberalism, shorn of its traditional attachment to the state.

Distributive justice and the problem of dominance

Theorists of the politics of identity build upon a communitarian concern with the idea of the liberal subject as denying the social constitution of personality and its consequent implications for moral and political philosophy. This can take a number of forms: either abandoning the communitarian advocacy of traditional social practices and identity-conferring institutions or affirming traditional identity-conferring practices and institutions, though acknowledging their plasticity. Developing the idea of personality and identity as a social creation, the multiculturalist identity theorist extends this idea into a critique of the character of contemporary liberal theories of justice because of their implicit individualism and tendency to universalism. This radical variant of multiculturalism, linking the problem of exclusionary norms of integration with the hegemony of the distributive paradigm in liberal political theory, is illustrated in the work of a number of pluralist critics of liberalism, such as Walzer, Young, Tully and Parekh. All these theorists differ in important respects; Walzer for example is not explicitly a multiculturalist at all, and Young is hostile to the kind of ethnic nationalism that lies at the heart of much multiculturalism. That said, the pluralist preoccupation with dominance and structural inequalities of power replicated in liberal theories of justice is shared by all of them. It is theorized most clearly in Walzer and Young, and thus much of this section will focus on their theories.

Walzer's work has an ambiguous character in that he can be conceived of as both a narrow communitarian in his attempt to replace political philosophy with situated social criticism,[4] and as a more radical pluralist critic regarding the concern of post-Rawlsian political theory with issues of distributive justice. It is in his latter guise that Walzer connects with the work of Iris Marion Young.[5]

Walzer's *Spheres of Justice* is an attempt to displace the so-called distributive paradigm which has come to hold centre stage since Rawls' *A Theory of Justice*. The distributive paradigm assumes, according to Walzer, that the fundamental issues of political theory are distributive in character; they involve some institution giving something – rights, basic liberties, etc. – to another group that does not have them. The goods that are being distributed are also supposed to have a universal character, like Rawls' primary goods. These are things people must want regardless of anything else they may want. For Walzer, conceiving all fundamental political issues as primarily distributive has negative political consequences. First, it assumes that there is some set of goods that all people want whatever else they want. This in turn entails a uniformity of human nature and moral agency, and a denial of cultural difference and social pluralism. Furthermore, it entails that cultural differences are of secondary importance, merely adding local colour to an essential universal nature. Second, the distributive approach assumes that the character and value of the goods that are to be distributed is uncontroversial. And, third, it assumes the need for a distributive agency whose responsibility it is to maintain and enact this distribution. It is this third idea that supports the centrality of the state in liberal theorizing about justice.

Walzer challenges the first two implications of the distributive paradigm by contending that men are not passive recipients of goods that have their origin elsewhere, but rather that they are active in creating social meanings. What this means is that the value attached to any particular good or object to be distributed is not something that can be abstracted from the conditions that gave rise to its creation, or from the identities and self-understandings of those involved in the creative process. For Walzer, our identities as persons cannot be given independently of the processes and contexts in which we create and discover our identities. Furthermore, these identity-conferring institutions and practices, which give rise to the social meanings of those things we create, embody within them appropriate localized standards or criteria of distribution. The appropriate distributive criteria for any good is not some absolute egalitarian standard, but rather a criterion internal to the distributive sphere constituted by the social meaning of the object. Walzer argues that this explains why we use terms of disapproval to describe prostitution or the sale of political or ecclesiastical offices. These are goods the like of which should not be sold but distributed in accordance with affection and intimacy in the case of sexual relations, or with piety, orthodoxy or teaching authority in the case of ecclesiastical office. Each sphere of distribution of a good that has a determinate social meaning should be kept autonomous from any other: thus wealth should not become the sole distributive criterion for all goods, such as health care, education, sexual favours or political office. The theory of spheres reinforces both the pluralism of ends that people pursue and the plurality of associations that individuals identify with independently of the state.

Focusing on the distribution of some determined set of universally valued primary goods obscures the real problem that modern liberal theories of justice fail to acknowledge, and that is the need to maintain the autonomy of each distributive sphere. The distributive paradigm focuses on the problem of monopoly rather than that of dominance. What this means is that the distributive paradigm identifies one set of social goods and claims as the common currency for measuring the value and access to all other goods people can pursue. The problem with this is that the dominant good is able to assume the position of dominance or common currency only by being held in the hands of one particular social group. This can be either a faction or social class, or it can be an institutional dominance, such as that of the state over the claims of civil society. The liberal distributionists assume that the problem of dominance can be dealt with by tackling the issue of monopoly control. If that monopoly can be broken then justice will be achieved. But Walzer argues that tackling monopoly with a simple theory of distributive equality leaves the problem of dominance unaddressed. If we take the example of money as a dominant good, then the requirement of simple equality would be to distribute wealth within a society in a way that avoids everyone being denied goods that are dependent upon the possession of wealth as a condition of access. Simple equality fails to deny the dominant position of money as the sole relevant criterion for determining access to social goods such as health, education or employment. Complex equality on the other hand is not concerned with the simple equalization of holdings, but rather with the need to challenge the dominance of any particular good. In this way Walzer attempts to alter the focus of attention from 'who has what', to the issue of 'who has the power' to transform the social meaning of a good into an instrument whereby that good holds a position of dominance over the distribution of all other goods. By attacking the issue of dominance, the monopolistic holding of any particular good becomes less of a political issue.

A critique of the liberal preoccupation with distribution may seem of only tangential relevance to the issue of the multicultural critique of liberal theories of justice. However, the broad outlines of Walzer's argument are taken up and developed by Iris Marion Young into one of the most radical and penetrating assaults on the exclusionary character of ·liberal norms of impartiality and justice. Young is particularly concerned to employ the concept of dominance as the primary issue of political theory to support her argument for a politics of difference that accommodates the claims of group identity and challenges the central dominance of the liberal state. The liberal state imposes an individualistic and exclusionary conception of identity that contradicts the claims of race, class and gender. For Young, the issue of multiculturalism does not merely address the issue of assimilating ethnocultural groups or immigrant communities into the wider societal culture. Instead multiculturalism is about democratizing the societal culture to include all identity groups in the reconstitution of society. Young, like Walzer, is a political pluralist, seeing groups and associations other than the state as embodying political authority.

The problem addressed by Young is one that reduces the political concerns of identity groups into mere requests for a certain kind of good, which they do not have, and which they need from others in order to become equal according to some pre-given liberal norm.[6] In the case of gender politics, this idea of equality assumes a gender-neutral norm against which women's disadvantage can be measured. Yet such a neutral standard is not possible due to the persistence of patriarchal domination, which shapes the range of opportunities a society offers. If those opportunities reflect the gender structure of society, then simply equalizing them will not address the problem of gender inequality but will merely disguise it. Feminist political theorists argue that women do not need to be equalized with men – that is, brought up to a level at which they can be like men in male-gendered political and social structures. Women and other oppressed identity groups need to be empowered in order to be able to create institutions and opportunities that are determined by their own priorities and self-understandings. Thus recognition is as important as redistribution.[7] There is no neutral conception of equal opportunity sets that avoid replicating the structural inequalities of power and status that feminists identify as patriarchy. The political challenge of both feminism and multiculturalism is to expose the way in which liberalism's reliance on the state as a distributive mechanism ignores the way in which the state is implicated in reproducing patriarchy and cultural injustice. Unless the state itself is challenged and sovereignty pluralized, it will simply mirror the relationships of dominance and monopoly that pluralist multiculturalists find at the root of the distributive paradigm of modern liberalism.

Young connects her critique of the distributive paradigm of contemporary liberalism with a conception of the person that borrows from communitarianism. For her, individual identity is not something that is pre-given; rather it is something that we acquire from membership of different identity-conferring institutions and practices. Yet, whereas many communitarians use this kind of argument to reinforce traditional social and political structures, Young takes a more radical view. Our identities, she claims, are much more fluid than the traditional communitarians recognize; consequently we can be members of a variety of identity-conferring institutions at any one time. Recognizing this issue of difference and pluralism at the level of personality, and the forms of life from which personality is derived, challenges the simple essentialism of some versions of multiculturalism, but it also challenges the individualism of the liberal subject. The problem with liberalism is that it attempts to impose a false identity on people by bringing them under a non-neutral egalitarian norm that already privileges certain conceptions of identity and personality – the political culture of modern liberalism. Young's challenge to this hegemonic liberal culture makes her a multiculturalist, albeit in a different way from other multiculturalists such as Will Kymlicka. The problem of dominance manifests itself through the invisibility of such identity-confering groups, whether these be ethnocultural, social (such as class) or sexual (such as lesbian and gay). Young criticizes liberalism's tendency to address such issues of group difference in terms of simple equality or equalization. Such an approach always assumes within its norm of inclusion precisely what is at issue, and has the effect of marginalizing the genuine identities of individuals because, in so far as these are inconsistent with the dominant culture of liberalism, they are ruled off the agenda.[8] These marginalized identities, and the groups bearing them, are also disempowered by liberalism, for it does not take account of the oppression and marginalization they feel as a result of being excluded from the norm of liberal society. The liberal state, even when acting as the distributor of justice, is merely one further variant of group dominance that carries a particular view of identity and excludes the possibility of challenging the dominant conceptions of personality and well-being that are operationalized within liberal political theories. The liberal state threatens pluralism, rather than protecting it, by its imposition of a unitary identity.

The appropriate response to this problem, according to Young, is not the redistribution of some set of primary goods from those who have them to those who do not; instead, it involves a political challenge to the dominant conception of personality that underlies liberal norms of inclusion. And this can only be acheived by pluralizing the state and undermining the tendency of the liberal state to assume a monistic character. This involves not the distribution of equal rights, but the political representation of difference or group representation. It is this issue of group representation and its challenge to the monistic liberal state, rather than the issue of cultural relativism (that was addressed in the last chapter), that is often overlooked in discussions of multiculturalism. Yet it is precisely this feature of pluralist democracy that is taken up by theorists of the rights of indigenous people, such as Ivison, Patton and Sanders.[9] In this way, the presence of different identities would be able to disrupt the distributive paradigm and exercise power in ways that allow these systematically oppressed groups to articulate and democratically negotiate their own political agendas. What needs to be equalized is recognition, rather than sets of preinterpreted primary goods. Recognition is precisely something that cannot be conferred in a top-down fashion, from a monistic liberal state; instead, if it is not to be a further manifestation of dominance, it must emerge through democratic negotiation.

According to the radical pluralist critique, the whole distributionist agenda of modern liberalism replicates the tyranny of the modern state over the equal recognition of other authoritative forms of democratic community. Thus, while impartialist liberals do not say much about the centrality of the state to their political agenda, it remains in the background casting a long shadow over political liberalism. The idea of protected rights and liberties conferred by a constitution that sets limits to the claims of the political is clearly at the heart of the approach we have explored in this book. Similarly, the provision of economic justice through the distribution of resources is also something that implies a central and authoritative distributor that is above and beyond democratic negotiation. This must be so because, for liberals, it is this idea of the priority of justice that confers legitimacy on a democratic decision. The question that remains is whether this liberal reliance on the idea of a monistic state is as malign as the radical pluralists suggest. Furthermore, is it a position that they can consistently avoid occupying?

Defending the distributive paradigm and the liberal state

The answer to the first question above is, I hope, clear from what has gone before in this book. Liberal political theory is concerned with setting out the conditions under which a state can be said to be legitimate and just. The political liberal certainly does not accept the Hobbesian picture of the state (nor its twentieth-century Schmittian variant), where sovereignty is above question and can be exercised however the sovereign chooses. For contemporary political liberals, as for their classical predecessors from the time of John Locke, the task of liberal political theory has been to specify the conditions under which the exercise of state power is compatible with the prior obligation to respect the equal status of the person. The concept of state sovereignty is clearly central to liberal arguments, as political liberalism is a theory about how the state should be structured, but it is not obvious that that particular relationship implicates liberalism in an endorsement of narrow statism. The idea of the constitutional state that underlies liberalism is simply an institutional vehicle for delivering the goods of liberal politics. Whether this connection with the idea of monistic sovereign political power is sufficient to damn liberal political theory, as radical pluralists claim, will depend on their success in avoiding appeal to an authoritative and institutionalized criterion of inclusion. I will show two possibilities in this section: perhaps they do succeed in avoiding this liberal move, but at a damaging cost; alternatively, they do not succeed in this move and end up paralleling precisely the moves of the liberals towards a constitutionally constrained conception of politics.

The attempt to avoid appeal to a monistic conception of the political association is most clear in communitarian variants of multiculturalism, such as that offered by Parekh or Tully. Both address the authoritative political claims of organized religio-ethnic cultures or minority nations as part of a challenge to pluralize the liberal state. Their claim that liberalism is *sovereigntist* is similar to the charge of associationist pluralism of Maitland, Figgis and Laski in the early part of the twentieth century.[10] They differ from these classical pluralists in the way they envisage the character of the relevant associations, but they retain the idea that associations such as cultures and first nations have a claim to self-determination. This claim is derived from the value of these forms of communities as sources of identity and self-respect for their members. Communal membership is also a source of norms and structures of authority that are particular to and characteristic of such groups. The communitarian pluralists go on to claim that because the scope of norms and values are local or particular we can have no universal and external standards against which their internal conduct can be assessed. (We examined the epistemological basis of this claim in the previous chapter). Consequently, there is no basis for a liberal impartialist constitution to authoritatively arbitrate between the claims of associations, cultures or minority nations. Multiculturalist pluralists, such as Tully and Parekh, argue that we must therefore see the terms of cooperation as something that emerges from a process of democratic deliberation between groups, each regarded as being of equal status. However, we have no good reason to expect such groups as a matter of fact to be of equal bargaining power in any such deliberation. Therefore, they are only likely to replicate the existing balance of power in a society, one in which the operative public values of the majority will always win.[11] This domination of the existing distribution of power needs to be addressed, but it cannot be addressed by any process that takes the existing relations of power in society for granted. Politics cannot provide a solution to the problem of structural dominance if it simply reflects that dominance. To overcome this we have to constrain politics in a way that makes possible a fair procedure for deliberation. This process requires some reflection on the nature of a fair procedure, but it cannot at the same time confine that reflection to the internal standards, values and understandings of a cultural community. And this brings us back to the agenda of political liberalism, for we cannot simply rely on the authority of 'how we do things around here', because that authority is precisely what is at issue. Simply referring to the autonomy of spheres of justice, community or culture is no help. And to think that we can resolve this problem by political negotiation is either hopelessly naive or it simply begs the question, as one ends up building into one's conception of democratic deliberation precisely those procedural values the liberal is accused of endorsing as pre-political. Iris Young's politics of difference is also based on the claim that liberalism is profoundly anti-political, because it places the determination of norms of inclusion above politics, and, therefore, reinforces the dominance of liberal interests and values. She differs from communitarian multiculturalists such as Parekh and Tully (although they would reject the designation) because her conception of identity-conferring groups is broader, encompassing social movements as well as groups, and because she claims that membership or participation in identity-conferring groups is complex and overlapping, with no single group constituting our identity.

To reinforce the political resolution of problems of group inclusion, and to challenge domination, Young advocates the additional representation of identity-conferring groups that have been traditionally marginalized. In this she is at one with the other radical pluralists, such as multiculturalist communitarians Parekh and Tully. Yet her approach brings out in stark form the question of which groups should be afforded additional special representation, and which identity groups should be denied recognition altogether. Thus we have a problem about how groups should interact, but also a problem about the internal character of groups as such. Young, more than Tully or Parekh, is prepared to acknowledge that many social and cultural groups can be sites of oppression. But if we are to start distinguishing between cultural groups and identities, how do we do that and who decides what is or is not a non-oppressive social practice or cultural group? Clearly, this issue of the criteria of inclusion and recognition cannot be internal to any group or culture. After all, oppressive and discriminatory norms are often perfectly reasonable to members within identity groups who already accept their authority.[12] The question is whether anybody else should.

A clear illustration of the problem is provided by the way many traditional cultures and religious groups regard the role and status of women. So it seems that Young only wishes to empower those identity-conferring groups that are non-coercive in some way, presumably because they acknowledge the equal status of others. She clearly excludes what she calls ideological groups, such as Nazis and racists. Yet her account of why such groups should be excluded is weak because of her reliance on a social constructionist account of identity. If all identities are socially constructed, and all norms and values are merely internal to those identities, then we have no perspective from which we can begin to say one is superior to the other. Yet once we move to an external perspective, i.e., one that is not internal to an identity-conferring group, we are back with the problem that faced the liberal multiculturalists: who decides and on what criteria?

If she were to employ a disguised foundational commitment to equality then she runs up against the limitations of her approach to difference, which we have already discussed above. If on the other hand she adopts an inegalitarian principle, arbitrarily favouring some groups at the expense of others, merely on the basis of some preference, then she will not have a principled response to those who reject her preferences. In that case we just have struggle and conflict. Many of the theorists of agonistic politics that we saw in chapter 6 would endorse precisely this conclusion, in that they argue there is no alternative to conflict between incommensurable views of the world. For disillusioned post-Marxists this might be a perfectly respectable position to hold, but Young is concerned with emancipatory politics and not with a pessimistic reconciliation with things as they are. The liberal approach provides a way of stepping outside the internalist perspective of group identities and adopting a proceduralist approach to their institutional accommodation and reconciliation. But, most importantly, it provides an approach to accommodation and inclusion that does not merely shunt the problem of oppression from the relations between groups in a political community, to the relations between individuals and groups within a social group or culture. If groups are not to have the final say over how they may act in their own spheres, then it is unclear how we can avoid appeal to the primacy of liberal values of individual equality of concern and respect.

The radical pluralists, such as Walzer, Young, Tully and Parekh, dismiss liberal political theory on the grounds that it operates with a norm of inclusion that is dominating and insensitive to the identity-conferring practices of cultural and social groups, not least because of its ethical individualism. Yet, in criticizing liberal theories and advancing claims for the equality of groups and cultures, they open themselves to precisely the problem that liberal theories attempt to address through the idea of the constitutional state, namely the tyranny of faction and group identity. These are precisely the issues the modern constitutional liberal state is supposed to impartially arbitrate. Yet they provide no structure or account of how this task is supposed to be achieved, other than through an optimistic hope in pure politics. They are generally unprepared to acknowledge that individuals can be sacrificed to the good of community or culture, but they are unprepared to explain how and why that should be so, and why the claims of the individual always trump those of culture and community. If they wish to resist this problem, then they must appeal to a prior second-order rule that gives members a veto over the extent to which aspects of identity can be imposed both from outside a group and crucially from within a group. Providing such a norm of inclusion as a pre-liminary to any political interaction between these groups takes us back to the liberal agenda of the terms of fair co-operation, whatever the pluralists may argue to the contrary. Liberal political theories do not deny the value of identity-conferring groups and associations or the value of group membership, but they do rule out conferring upon those groups sovereign authority in dealing with their members. It is the institutional consequences of setting limits to the claims of groups that takes us towards the liberal ideal of the constitutional state. By divorcing political identity (citizenship) from group membership, and consequently treating each citizen as of equal value and status, liberalism provides a solution to the conflict of identity and belonging that unrestricted pluralism invites. This liberal conception of the constitutional state is a precarious achievement and is not something that should be dispensed with lightly.

Beyond the liberal state?

In the previous two sections of this chapter we have explored a challenge to liberalism's conception of the constitutional state. We have seen that the abandonment of the idea of a unified constitutional state in favour of a pluralist and fragmented sovereignty is unattractive, because of the way it merely tranfers the negative aspects of state sovereignty to cultural communities and social groups, thus displacing but not dispensing with issues of accountability and limitation. On the other hand, I have tried to show how the idea of the constitutional state as a site of political power can serve the normative purposes of liberalism. However, I need to make clear at this stage that the relationship between liberal values and principles, and the institutional structure of the liberal constitutional state, is still contingent. The fact that liberals tend to assume a set of institutions such as those of the constitutional state is not intended to entail that the scope of liberal principles and values will only apply within the territory and jurisdiction of a state. Liberals, as I have argued in chapter 7, are universalists and not particularists, even if some such as Rawls and Dworkin seem to veer towards a kind of particularism.[13] Liberal values are supposed to have a resonance and claim on all humans, wherever they happen to be. While the constitutional state was the only game in town, the connection of liberal values and state sovereignty was relatively unproblematic. However, it has become commonplace to argue that our traditional understanding of the state has been challenged by the facts of globalization, and, therefore, we need to reconceive the relationship between what I have called in this book liberal values and principles, and the state. If liberal values are connected with the state and the state is going through a process of profound transformation, what implication does this have for the concerns of liberalism? Second, is liberalism as a political theory being displaced by cosmopolitanism, which is the endorsement of liberal values outside of any connection to the institutional structures of the state?[14] As a conclusion to this book, I want to consider the prospects for liberalism in light of the challenge of globalization and the cosmopolitan turn.

Liberalism, cosmopolitanism and statism

An increasingly common strand of criticism of the kind of liberalism I have been defending is that it employs a naive domestic analogy of politics and distribution that only applies within contemporary state structures. As such, liberalism tends towards being a *statist*, or what international relations theorists often call a *realist*, ideology or theory. This view sees states as autonomous units that relate towards each other in a competitive struggle to secure their particular interests. These interests are specific to each state, and each state has a unique jurisdiction over the pursuit of its interests in its own territory. Between states, relations are shaped by contracts and agreements (treaties and alliances) that are governed by principles of mutual advantage.[15] There is supposed to be a division of labour between domestic politics, which can be about issues of justice, and the realm of international relations and politics, which is shaped by a different agenda of issues. The issue is whether liberalism is committed to such a statist view. The account I have given in this book seems to pull in two directions. First, the core of liberalism is described as comprising a set of universal moral commitments to the equal status of the person. This places constraints on how domestic political power can be exercised. Second, liberalism addresses the appropriate set of principles and institutions to secure the equal concern and respect of the person, in terms of a just basic structure and a state with constitutional constraints on power, together with redistributive institutions such as a well-resourced welfare system. The tension arises because the first commitment to equal moral concern is universal in scope and, therefore, does not merely apply to those with whom we are engaged in social cooperation. This moral concern does not cease at Dover, or any other port! Yet clearly the provisions of justice and equal treatment, as they follow from a set of institutions, do cease at some particular place – perhaps the state borders. My obligations to support the welfare of British citizens through the taxation system are different from obligations I might have towards the French or Chinese. The question is whether these differences of obligation mark an institutional division of labour or a recognition of genuinely different obligations.[16] Particularists argue that obligations of justice run out at the boundaries of the state, and we are left with something thinner and less urgent beyond the state. Statism as an ideology or theory seems to map on to the particularist approach very well. Yet this particularist approach is precisely the one I have contested in relation to the radical pluralist critique of liberal theories of justice and the state. This is because, if we concede particularism in relation to the state, there is no good argument against those who make parallel claims for sub-state groups such as nations and cultures. The good arguments against the ethical significance of nationality and culture are arguments against particularism itself and not merely about broadening its scope.

The liberal objection to statism is not merely an objection to the theoretical underpinning of ethical particularism. Liberals, as universalists, are compelled by their principles and values to be concerned about injustice wherever it occurs. For this reason many liberals also describe themselves as cosmopolitans, and many liberals are as concerned in their writings with issues of global distributive justice, and the terms of intervention to secure human rights against violations, as they are about transforming the distribution of resources within states. Indeed, many cosmopolitan liberals would argue that this turn towards the global is not merely a new current of intellectual fashion, but is actually a pre-condition of thinking about justice in the state itself. After all, inequalities and injustices within states are often highly relative (though not insignificant), so that the differences between richest and poorest in Switzerland or Norway might seem minor in comparison to those between the worst off in Norway and the worst off in a sub-Saharan African state such as Chad or Niger. Until we deal with the issue of inequality between states and regions of the world we cannot establish a base-line from which to begin thinking about the level of equal resources needed to create just equal opportunity sets within a state. Furthermore, if liberals are genuinely concerned about respecting basic rights and liberties, and challenging their violation or denial, then it is not clear why liberals as universalists should be interested in the historical contingencies of national borders as a legitimate limitation on jurisdiction and concern for rights violations. These two questions, of global justice and intervention to protect human rights, challenge the primacy of the state in liberal thinking, and support a more cosmopolitan approach that separates liberals' universal values from the institutional questions of how these values are put into practice. Does this mean that the liberal focus on the basic structure of society and the state is redundant – that is, that liberalism focuses on the wrong site of justice?

The first thing to say in response to this challenge is to emphasize that the connection between liberalism and the state is contingent. The form of liberalism I have been describing and defending in this book is cosmopolitan in that the scope of its core values is universal, as we saw in chapter 7. This approach sees the state as an institutional vehicle for realizing these universal values and goals; as such we can avoid liberalism being seen as a crude statist theory. But that said, I want to argue that one must not make too quick a move from the contingency of state in liberal theory to its irrelevance or redundancy.

If we draw a distinction between ideal and non-ideal theory, we can see the relation between liberal theory and the state. At the level of ideal theory, the issue of just social relations is dealt with in all political communities in broadly the same way.[17] Thus all individuals, wherever they happen to be, are secured equal concern and respect in whichever state or political community they find themselves. That they are members of one state rather than another is irrelevant because all states respect their members equally, and, as they are impartial between individuals, they would accord similar conditions of concern and respect to non-citizens who fall under their jurisdiction because of travel or relocation. Citizenship in this sense would be a universal category, but one administered in particular institutions – i.e. states. But, as these states would not appeal to particular and contingent features of people, citizens would enjoy the same status wherever they happened to be. Nothing significant would follow from being a United Kingdom citizen or a Chinese citizen, other than which state takes first reponsibility for delivering services of justice such as health care and education. For liberals, under ideal conditions, the rights of citizenship of one country should be no less eligible than those of any other. In this respect equality of concern and respect, or equal protection of the law, would be achieved in a regime of states. Only in this ideal respect is liberalism a straightforwardly 'statist' theory. It is certainly not a realist approach as traditionally understood in international relations theory because it does not accord unlimited sovereignty to the state, as the state may only do that which is legitimate in terms of the prior criteria of liberal justice. Issues of war and compliance would only arise in the circumstances of non-ideal theory, where not all states are justly ordered or prepared to act according to universal principles of justice.

Before turning to this issue, it is worth briefly considering why liberalism as an ideal theory does not simply defend a universal single political community. If we are part of a universal moral community (as cosmopolitanism asserts), why not have a single world state or global political community? The answer to this question goes back to the heart of liberalism as a way of accommodating disagreements between individuals and groups over how to live. As individuals and group members have conflicting motivations and aspirations, the desire to act on liberal principles will often conflict with the desire to pursue other ends, even though the obligation is primary. In order to sustain the priority of liberal obligations, they need to be enforced, especially when there is potential conflict between groups of individuals. As liberalism offers a limited conception of politics that rejects the idea of achieving human redemption on earth through political means, disagreement will persist. Liberals, therefore, need some institutional and political structures which enforce liberal principles and rights and arbitrate in cases of potential conflict. That is what the liberal constitutional state is for. In order to be successful at this, liberals argue that such compliance mechanisms and adjudicative structures need to be relatively close to those to whom they apply, as this allows them to be more efficient and less forceful in their exercise of coercion. And, what is of equal importance, this relative proximity allows citizens to hold the exercise of political power accountable. If the state is too big it risks being ineffective, but also distant and unaccountable. This Hobbesian insight into why there is no world state or sovereign power is sufficiently uncontroversial that a version of it is to be found in the principle of proximity or subsidiarity, deployed by more radical cosmopolitan democrats such as David Held, who is sympathetic to some conception of global governance, though not a world state.[18] A fully cosmopolitan argument for a global state or community that was not simply a loose confederation would have to advance a substantive ethic of the sort political liberals wish to avoid. Thus there remain good arguments as to why we should have proximate political institutions to achieve liberal goals.

The question that remains is how this liberal ideal maps on to the reality of contemporary politics. This takes us into the realm of non-ideal theory, or how liberal principles and values should be applied given the circumstances of the world as they are and the fact that many states are not liberal and show little immediate prospect of acknowledging liberal values. It is at this level that we come back to the questions of global justice and intervention to prevent the gross violation of human rights.

The first obvious constraint on liberal ideal theory is the current global distribution of resources. There are huge differences in economic wealth between states. Many of these arise from contingent historical factors, which are accompanied by historical injustices. Borders were often drawn precisely to exclude others from access to resource wealth.

Other factors are merely a matter of luck, such as the distribution of oil or other mineral deposits. Before we can begin to consider moving towards a liberal ideal we need to address these pressing issues of global inequality. Until some kind of global baseline is attained, the issue of the just distribution of resources within any one state is beside the point. The second issue concerns compliance with liberal values or basic human rights, and what to do when these are grossly violated. Here the liberal is again in the situation of challenging current UN Charter Articles 2–7 that protect states from intervention on matters that are purely within their jurisdiction. This protection is often used for turning a blind eye towards human rights abuses within states. Yet, if persons are due equal concern and respect, no issue of state borders can trump the enjoyment of their rights. This does not of course directly entail a duty to intervene, as we need clear rules about who should intervene, and when, in order to preclude merely arbitrary and advantageous interventions to support rights and equality.[19] But these are practicalities and do not support the claim that states have any more of a free hand within their borders than sub-state communities have in coercing their members.

The question that remains is what do both of these considerations entail? In practice they entail a significant challenge to the current regime of states as enshrined in United Nations Declarations and Covenants. Ironically, they do entail a more cosmopolitan arrangement than the ideal liberal model I sketched above, not least because the threats to liberal goals from illiberal states are considerably greater concerns than the issues of accountability and proximity that are entailed by a liberal view of a world of constitutional states. Yet both of these considerations are different. The problem of non-compliance directs us towards institutional structures for common defence, the regulation of the use of force, and the circumstances where intervention is required. This takes us into the realm of international institutions for an international order among states – a way of regulating statism to bring it towards the ideal of a just system of states. It is in principle possible to see this as part of a process towards an end result that is not incompatible with the liberal ideal. Yet the constraint of global justice is ineradicable, as there can be no one-off redistribution that establishes an ideal baseline of fairness between states. Does this fact challenge the adequacy of the liberal model? It certainly requires the establishment of some structures of redistribution that exist over and above the state or proximate political community, in order to collect and coordinate the transfer of resources. This would be so even if we could overcome the problem of compliance, or of making states see the urgency of global justice, which is the more pressing practical concern in contemporary politics. But even if we do persuade all states to accept the obligations of global justice, we would need structures to put that agreed agenda into practice. This would not, as I say, be a temporary measure. Consequently, drawing a distinction between ideal and non-ideal theory does not necessarily save liberalism from the charge of redundancy as a result of its residual statism.

The ineradicability of the global features of modern politics have led some thinkers, such as Held and McGrew, or Singer, to seek a more global form of governance that overcomes the statism of even ideal liberal politics.[20] Although their arguments are different, they focus on the contingency of the modern state system and the need to separate the universal values I have associated with liberalism from a particular institutional structure, such as the state. This is not merely because of the problem of non-compliance, but because of a significant, or according to Held and McGrew, qualitative transformation of world politics as a result of the phenomenon of globalization.[21] The scale and reach of global interdependence has, we are told, transformed the world and set in train new political problems that cannot be encompassed within the state system, even purged of its residual Hobbesian notion of sovereign autonomy. State and national borders are not simply seen as arbitrary boundaries around people who are universal citizens, but they are increasingly inadequate to contain and therefore discipline transnational actors such as global economic institutions. Instead of a unitary model of state power, however we try to purge it of its Hobbesian legacy, we need a pluralized, overlapping and complex interrelation of different levels of democratic accountability. This tendency towards a cosmopolitan democracy builds on some familiar ideas about universal equal status and the denial of any moral priority to contingencies of history such as nationality. As Singer writes of the need to cede increasing power and authority to international institutions such as the World Trade Organization (suitably modified), the International Labour Organization and UNESCO, all as part of moving towards a complex regime of global governance, so Held is concerned with the issue of democratization of these new institutions of global governance. The analysis of global politics offered in these cosmopolitan theories is subtle and comprehensive, and it covers precisely those issues of global injustice that liberal theory is supposed to ignore. This attempt to reconnect the aspirations of universalist egalitarian political theory with a more nuanced account of politics does mark a change in direction in political theory away from the narrowly domestic concerns of some liberal theories, which seem to assume that the only issue in politics is the level of taxation and the structure of the welfare state. Cosmopolitan theories of global governance and democracy mark a refreshing change of direction. The question with which I want to conclude is whether they displace liberalism and its residual connection with the state. My answer is that, as yet, an ideal liberal statist model can still prove a useful paradigm for thinking about the issues of global politics, even in an age of globalization.

It is important to re-emphasize that this is not a simplistic endorsement of statism as the so-called morality of modern international realism – that is, states pursuing their autonomous interests with no external rules constraining what can count as the interest of a state. As I have already mentioned, the liberal model is not an endorsement of a Hobbesian model, because it recognizes only the claims of rightly organized states – that is, states which have a just constitution and basic structure. Therefore, in so far as there is a residual claim for sovereignty within the liberal model, it is conditional upon that sovereignty being rightly constituted and exercised. This right constitution and exercise depends also upon a recognition of the claims of global distributive justice and the rule of law-governed institutions for responding to non-compliance with liberal norms, escalating up to the level of military intervention for the most gross violations of human rights such as the threat of genocide and ethnic cleansing. As all rightly ordered states will be structurally similar in their basic constitution, the claims of state sovereignty are considerably weakened. In this way even the liberal ideal, although it retains a connection with a version of the modern juridical or constitutional state, nevertheless comprises a significant development from the idea of the sovereign state that emerged in the sixteenth century with Hobbes and Bodin. Yet this concession does not go as far as the cosmopolitan democrats suggest, and the reason for this has to do with the liberals' suspicion of the value of political pluralism or international pluralism. As we saw in the case of internal state pluralism, the problem is merely one of the displacement of decision-making power from one site to another, making sub-state groups sovereign. Similarly, in the case of global pluralism, liberals fear the tendency of displaced decision-making power to new sites that exercise sovereign power at too great a remove from popular accountability. If there is vertical pluralism, then we replicate the problem of imperialism or parochialism that the modern state (in its ideal form) was supposed to overcome. Higher authorities must be held accountable in the right way, but accountable by and to whom? This can be achieved in a top-down or a bottom-up way. If one thinks of the emergence of the idea of subsidiarity in medieval ecclesiology, this is a classic example of the centre conferring power down to more local level (from popes to bishops for example), in order to better secure the good determined by the centre. Bottom-up accountability would confer authority on a level above the state to achieve some common good, such as international regulation. But here the source of authority is local and not that of a central authority. As we have seen, the liberal model seeks a universal content to an account of state legitimacy, but leaves the source of political authority functionally local in order to better hold it accountable. If on the other hand the pluralization of the global realm is horizontal, then it must map on to something like the ideal of a modified liberal statism. Rightly conceived, the issue between the liberal and the cosmopolitan is not one concerning the character of the goods of politics. Both are individualistic in an ethical sense and both are universalistic in this commitment.

The key difference concerns how best to secure these liberal or cosmopolitan goals (at this level of theory the terms are interchangeable). Liberalism retains a practical scepticism about the demands of public morality because of the need to accommodate ends which are reasonable but irreducibly conflicting. This demands, as a matter of institutional design, that sites of power are sufficiently close to be held accountable and to be effective with minimal coercion. The further these sites are from us, the weaker their claims upon us. This is an argument for proximity, not for subsidiarity, although it is challenging for the liberal because it does mean that issues arise regarding the possibility of a maximum size for a genuinely liberal state. Although liberals do not swallow whole the Hobbesian conception of sovereignty that cosmopolitan democrats reject, they retain a commitment to a site of legitimate decision-making. This must reappear somewhere in any viable account of the polity, however large one imagines it to be, if we are to avoid chaos. What liberalism offers us is a way of conceiving this residual sovereign power in terms of what would make its exercise legitimate. As the answer to that question has a universal content, the liberal theory draws the sting out of the normative concerns raised by cosmopolitans about the concept of sovereignty. This means that the real debate between liberals and cosmopolitans is primarily institutional and not normative. And on this question the issues cannot be settled by normative political theory, but must draw upon political science and social psychology. What is clear is that the liberal commitment to the state is not such as to make it practically redundant in the face of multiculturalism or globalization, nor is it normatively redundant in the face of cosmopolitanism, because at the appropriate level of generality the two are identical.

Conclusion

I began this book with the claim that liberalism is a precarious achievement. This is increasingly borne out in the contemporary politics of Atlantic democracies, which seek to abandon and trim the liberal ideal that I have outlined. While for many, this will mean that the liberal vision is increasingly redundant, I would like to conclude the defence of liberalism by arguing that the prosecution case is not proven. The current fashions of political practice prove nothing other than the need to heed ideas, which though familiar have lost none of their value and urgency. The main challenges offered by the academy are also far from fatal. Many of them simply trade on ideas and conceptual distinctions that are no more secure than those deployed in liberal argument. I do not, however, intend to imply that liberalism claims the field and sees off all its challengers. There are still vital questions of central importance for liberal theory, such as intergenerational justice, environmental duties and issues of global justice. Liberals are no more settled on answers to these questions than are non-liberals. But that is to be expected, and not a fatal concern for the argument as set out in this book. How the approach sketched out here is to be extended and applied is a complex question, but that there are still questions to address is a sign of the vitality rather than the redundancy of an approach to politics. It would be problematic if liberalism clearly had nothing left to say, as then it would be an outmoded political form. So the account of liberalism set out in this book is inevitably incomplete. That said, it should be clear that liberalism does not simply entail the abandonment of politics properly conceived; neither does it entail a simplistic cultural imperialism or ethnocentricity. Most importantly, the liberal vision of the state is neither a simple endorsement of the practices of actually existing states, nor is it something we should abandon lightly. Although the world certainly differs from 1651 and Hobbes' *Leviathan*, it does not differ so much that we can dispense with all the lessons of the chequered history of the modern state. In many parts of the world, far from needing to transcend the state, building states is precisely what we need to do. But we need to do that in a particular way. Simply moving sites of injustice and tyranny is no great achievement. The states we want and need are liberal states, and these are very different from all actually existing states. The key issue is their liberal character, not their holding a monoply of violence in a territory – although that is often useful to secure liberal goals. But if this model of the state is so far removed from actual practice is not the liberal project just hopelessly utopian?

Clearly, I think that the liberal project is not hopelessly utopian, but equally I do not adopt the caricature opposite view that liberalism is simply a rationalistic blueprint, imposed by hubristic academics who cannot exercise power directly. It is for political scientists, sociologists and policy-makers to translate theory into practice. It is not the task of political theorists to address every fine detail of institutional design. Yet normative political theory has an important purpose. That purpose is to explore, challenge and defend ideas that are the common currency of our politics. In so doing it does not merely explore what societies actually think they are about, but also explores questions about what they should be about. We need such theories so that none of those closer to power can get away with claims that structures of inequality of wealth and power are not merely difficult to change, but are in some sense morally desirable. The task of political analysis and criticism depends also on the reconstruction and theorizing of other sets of values and principles. This necessary task forms the area into which the articulation and defence of liberalism falls. The simple opposition between realist and rationalist forces the task of political theory on to a Procrustean bed. Yet it is by no means clear that political theory needs to fall under one or other category. Fortunately for political liberalism, things are never quite so simple. If we reject this simple opposition we can salvage a space for liberal theory. As an activity it does not rest on a category mistake or some misunderstanding of the nature of politics. What further value it has in challenging dominant discourses of political justification will depend upon its powers to challenge the assumptions of rival views.

The poet Robert Frost is credited with the claim that a liberal is someone who cannot take his own side in an argument (no book on liberalism would be complete without a repetition of Frost's aphorism). This misunderstanding trades on the idea that toleration and accommodation are at the heart of liberal politics. That much is true, but it is simply a mistake to think that liberalism amounts to no more than a disposition to be tolerant. Liberalism, as much as any other theory, can be given a clear and defensible content. It is no less of a fighting creed than any other political theory. What I hope to have shown is that there is more than enough to political liberalism on which one can, and indeed should, take a stand.

Notes

Chapter 1 Introduction: What is Liberalism?

1 See J. Gray, *Liberalism*, Milton Keynes, Open University Press, 1984; *Enlightenment's Wake*, London, Routledge, 1995; and, most recently, *Two Faces of Liberalism*, Cambridge, Polity, 2000. Yet Gray is not alone: see also A. Arblaster, *The Rise and Decline of Western Liberalism*, Oxford, Blackwell, 1984; P. Neal, *Liberalism's Discontents*, Basingstoke, Macmillan, 1997; A. MacIntyre, *After Virtue*, London, Duckworth, 1981; M. Sandel, *Democracy's Discontent*, Cambridge, MA, Harvard University Press, 1995; R. Beiner, *What's the Matter with Liberalism?*, Berkeley, CA, University of California Press, 1992; and G. Newey, *After Politics*, Basingstoke, Palgrave, 2000.

2 See especially the work of Quentin Skinner in *Visions of Politics*, vol 1, *Regarding Method*, Cambridge, Cambridge University Press, 2002.

3 For a different, more sociological account, see John A. Hall, *Liberalism*, London, Paladin, 1987.

4 J. Gray, *Endgames: Questions in Late Modern Political Theory*, Cambridge, Polity, 1997.

5 These views can be found in: John Dunn, *Western Political Theory in the Face of the Future*, Cambridge, Cambridge University Press, 1977; Francis Fukuyama, *The End of History and the Last Man*, New York, Free Press, 1992; and R. Geuss, *History and Illusion*, Cambridge, Cambridge University Press, 2000.

6   See P. Kelly, 'Political Theory in Retreat? Contemporary Political Philosophy and the Historical Order', in Noel O'Sullivan (ed.), *Political Theory in Transition*, London, Routledge, 2000, pp. 225–41.

7   R. Dworkin, 'Liberalism', in *A Matter of Principle*, Oxford, Oxford University Press, 1985, pp. 181–204.

8   See J. S. Mill, 'On Liberty', in *John Stuart Mill On Liberty and Other Essays*, J. Gray (ed.), Oxford, Oxford University Press, 1991.

9   See J. Raz *The Morality of Freedom*, Oxford, Clarendon Press, 1984. For the discussion of the ambiguities of equality as a value, see L. Temkin, *Inequality*, Oxford, Oxford University Press, 1993.

10 For a forthright defence of this aspect of liberal egalitarianism see the work of Jeremy Waldron, especially *Liberal Rights*, Cambridge, Cambridge University Press, 1988.

11 Some critics, most notably Alasdair MacIntrye in his book *After Virtue*, London, Duckworth, 1981, claim that liberals must be committed to moral scepticism, or what he calls emotivism, and atomism. This book argues that he is wrong on both counts.

12 G. Newey, *After Politics*, Basingstoke, Palgrave, 2001.

13 B. Parekh, *Rethinking Multiculturalism*, Basingstoke, Macmillan, 2000.

14 Q. Skinner, *Liberty Before Liberalism*, Cambridge, Cambridge University Press, 1998; and J. Tully, *Strange Multiplicity*, Cambridge, Cambridge University Press, 1995.

15 D. Held and A. McGrew, *Globalization/Anti-Globalization*, Cambridge, Polity, 2002; and P. Singer, *One World*, New Haven, Yale University Press, 2002.

16 J. S. Mill, 'On Liberty', in *John Stuart Mill On Liberty and Other Essays*, J. Gray (ed.), Oxford, Oxford University Press, 1991, pp. 20–61.

Chapter 2   The Sources of Liberal Equality

1   I use the term contractualist, rather than contractarian, because it is broader and covers both contract theories of political sovereignty and consent theories of political obligation, as well as more recent attempts to account for moral authority in terms of hypothetical agreements. Although different, all three approaches have important similarities and connections. See my 'Contractarian Ethics', in *Encyclopaedia of Applied*

Ethics, vol. 1, San Diego, Academic Press, 1997, pp. 631–43, and P. Kelly and D. Boucher, 'The Social Contract and Its Critics', in P. Kelly and D. Boucher (eds), *The Social Contract From Hobbes to Rawls*, London, Routledge, 1994, pp. 1–34.

2   For a discussion of contractarian theories of justice, see my 'Contractarian Social Justice: An Overview of Some Contemporary Debates', in D. Boucher and Paul Kelly (eds), *Social Justice from Hume to Walzer*, London, Routledge, 1998, pp. 181–99.

3   A. Smith, *The Theory of Moral Sentiments* (1759), eds D. D. Raphael and A. L. Macfie, Oxford, Clarendon Press, 1976; the ideal of the impartial spectator is reprieved in Hare's character of the Archangel in R. M. Hare, *Moral Thinking: Its Method, Levels and Point*, Oxford, Clarendon Press, 1981.

4   See O. O'Neill, *Contructions of Reason*, Cambridge, Cambridge University Press, 1989; and C. M. Korsgaard, *The Sources of Normativity*, Cambridge, Cambridge University Press, 1996.

5   T. Hobbes, *Leviathan*, (1651), ch. 14, ed. R. Tuck, Cambridge, Cambridge University Press, 1996, p. 92.

6   The most important recent attempt to use a 'Hobbesian' argument to ground moral norms is provided in D. Gauthier, *Morals by Agreement*, Oxford, Clarendon Press, 1986. For a discussion and critique of Gauthier's argument, see B. Barry, *Justice as Impartiality*, Oxford, Clarendon Press, 1995, and the essays in P. Kelly, *Impartiality, Neutrality and Justice*, Edinburgh, Edinburgh University Press, 1998.

7   Recent recoveries of Hobbes as a sceptical or *agonistic* liberal can be found in R. E. Flathman, *Thomas Hobbes: Skepticism, Individuality and Chastened Politics*, Thousand Oaks, CA, Sage, 1994, and John Gray, *Two Faces of Liberalism*, Cambridge, Polity, 2000.

8   See especially the work of John Dunn and Ian Harris: J. Dunn, *The Political Thought of John Locke: An Historical Account of the Argument of the Two Treatises of Government*, Cambridge, Cambridge University Press, 1969, and *Locke*, Oxford, Oxford University Press, 1984; and Ian Harris, *The Mind of John Locke*, Cambridge, Cambridge University Press, 1994. For an important corrective and analysis of the significance of Locke for liberal egalitarianism, see Jeremy Waldron, *God, Locke and Equality*, Cambridge, Cambridge University Press, 2002.

9   J. Locke, *Two Treatises of Government* (1689), ed. P. Laslett, Cambridge, Cambridge University Press, 1970. For an interesting defence of Locke's account of fundamental equality, coupled with the controversial idea that an adequate

defence of fundamental equality does in the end depend upon a theological (or specifically Christian) basis, see Jeremy Waldron, *God, Locke and Equality*, Cambridge, Cambridge University Press, 2002. See also J. E. Coons and P. M. Berman, *By Nature Equal*, Princeton, Princeton University Press, 1999.

10 J. Locke, *An Essay Concerning Human Understanding*, ed. P. H. Nidditch, Oxford, Clarendon Press, 1975.

11 P. Kelly and D. Boucher, 'The Social Contract and its Critics', in Boucher and Kelly (eds), *The Social Contract From Hobbes to Rawls*, London, Routledge, 1994, pp. 1–34.

12 For a critique of this view of morality, see B. Williams, *Ethics and the Limits of Philosophy*, London, Fontana, 1986, and A. MacIntyre, *After Virtue*, London, Duckworth, 1981. Both Williams and MacIntyre argue that this conception of morality is historically contingent rather than universal and transhistorical. However, they both draw different historical conclusions from this contingency. For a recent discussion of some of these issues, see J. Raz, *The Practice of Value*, Oxford, Clarendon Press, 2003.

13 T. M. Scanlon, 'Contractualism and Utilitarianism', in A. Sen and B. Williams (eds), *Utilitarianism and Beyond*, Cambridge, Cambridge University Press, 1982, pp. 103–28; and Brian Barry, *Justice as Impartiality*, Oxford, Clarendon Press, 1995. Scanlon has since developed a more complex account of moral motivation in *What We Owe to Each Other*, Cambridge, MA, Belknap/Harvard University Press, 1999.

14 For a more sophisticated account of Bentham's utilitarian theory, see P. Kelly, *Utilitarianism and Distributive Justice: Jeremy Bentham and the Civil Law*, Oxford, Clarendon Press, 1990; and for John Stuart Mill, see F. Berger, *Happiness, Justice and Freedom*, Berkeley, CA, University of California Press, 1984.

15 A. Smith, *The Theory of Moral Sentiments*, ed. D. D. Raphael and A. L. Macfie, Oxford, Clarendon Press, 1976.

16 R. M. Hare, *Moral Thinking: Its Method, Levels and Point*, Oxford, Clarendon Press, 1981, pp. 44–64.

17 Quoted in J. S. Mill, *Utilitarianism*, in J. S., Mill, *On Liberty and Other Essays*, ed. J. Gray, Oxford, Oxford University Press, 1991, p. 199.

Chapter 3 The Social Contract

1 R. Barker, *Political Legitimacy and the State*, Oxford, Clarendon Press, 1990 and *Legitimating Identities*, Cambridge, Cambridge University Press, 2001.

2 J. Rawls, *A Theory of Justice* (revised edn), Oxford, Oxford University Press, 1999, p. 3.

3 R. Dworkin, *Taking Rights Seriously*, London, Duckworth, 1977, p. 151.

4 Dworkin goes on to develop a more complex understanding of liberal justification, which tries to steer a middle course between contractualism and communitarianism, in his Tanner Lectures. However, even here, he retains the idea of 'endorsement' or reasonable agreement as a central liberal building block of his argument, and it is this that connects his approach with the contract vision of political association. See R. Dworkin, 'Foundations of Liberal Egalitarianism', in G. B. Peterson (ed.), *The Tanner Lectures on Human Values*, vol. xi, Salt Lake City, University of Utah Press, 1990.

5 Many critics of Rawls have argued that he does presuppose the value of equality but that his contractarian and individualistic account of equality actually undermines egalitarianism. This argument is most forcefully advanced by Gerry Cohen: see G. A. Cohen, 'Where the Action Is: On the Site of Distributive Justice', *Philosophy and Public Affairs*, 26 (1997), 3–30. Yet it is crucial that Rawls and contractarian liberals provide a procedural conception of equality, for to advance a substantive conception of equality risks begging the question with which contemporary liberals start, namely the fact of reasonable disagreement. It might well be the case that Rawls is wrong in his account of what egalitarianism requires, as many contractarian liberals also claim. However, a critique of contractarian liberalism on the basis of a controversial substantive conception of equality misunderstands the limitations within which normative theories must operate, in a world characterized by reasonable disagreement.

6 B. Barry, 'How Not to Defend Liberal Institutions', in R. Bruce Douglass, G. M. Mara and H. S. Richardson (eds), *Liberalism and the Good*, New York, Routledge, 1990.

7 The idea that liberalism rests on a conception of false neutrality is an important source of criticism and major preoccupation of contemporary political theory. It is potentially the most damaging criticism of liberalism and so will be addressed in more detail in chapter 7.

8 B. Barry, *Justice as Impartiality*, Oxford, Clarendon Press, 1995; see also P. Kelly (ed.), *Impartiality, Neutrality and Justice*. Edinburgh, Edinburgh University Press, 1998.

9 J. Rawls, *A Theory of Justice*, Oxford, Oxford University Press, 1999, p. 11.

10   For a libertarian critique, see R. Nozick, *Anarchy, State and Utopia*, Oxford, Blackwell, 1974; and for the communitarians, see M. Sandel, *Liberalism and the Limits of Justice*, Cambridge, Cambridge University Press, 1982.

11   Rawls goes to considerable pains to argue that his contract theory does not fall foul of this standard challenge to traditional social contract arguments. See especially, John Rawls, *Political Liberalism*, New York, Columbia University Press, 1993, pp. 285–88.

12   B. Barry, 'Something in the Disputation not Unpleasant', in P. Kelly (ed.), *Impartiality, Neutrality and Justice*, Edinburgh, Edinburgh University Press, 1998, pp. 186–200.

13   T. M. Scanlon, 'Contractualism and Utilitarianism', in A. Sen and B. Williams (eds), *Utilitarianism and Beyond*, Cambridge, Cambridge University Press, 1982, p. 104.

14   Indeed, in his second book *Political Liberalism*, New York, Columbia University Press, 1993, Rawls has come to play down the idea of choice in the original position and behind the veil of ignorance as merely devices for representing the more important components of his theory of justice as fairness.

15   Especially in practical deliberation within civil society. For a good overview of Locke's theory, see J. Waldron, 'John Locke', in D. Boucher and P. Kelly (eds), *Political Thinkers*, Oxford, Oxford University Press, 2003, pp. 181–97.

16   This argument is made most forcefully by Bernard Williams against act-utilitarianism, in B. Williams, 'A Critique of Utilitarianism', in B. Williams and J. J. C. Smart (eds), *Utilitarianism: For and Against*, Cambridge, Cambridge University Press, 1973. Williams extends his argument against Kantianism in B. Williams, *Ethics and the Limits of Philosophy*, London, Fontana, 1985. For a critique of Barry's response to Williams, see S. Mendus, 'Some Mistakes about Impartiality', in P. Kelly (ed.), *Impartiality, Neutrality and Justice*, Edinburgh, Edinburgh University Press, 1998, pp. 176–85.

17   R. Nozick, *Anarchy, State and Utopia*, Oxford, Blackwell, 1974; and H. Steiner, *An Essay on Rights*, Oxford, Blackwell, 1995. Nozick and Steiner have very different libertarian theories, but they are united in the important respect that their accounts of basic rights exhaust the realm of morality and politics.

18   R. Dworkin, *Taking Rights Seriously*, London, Duckworth, 1977, and *A Matter of Principle*, Oxford, Oxford University

Press, 1985. In his later works it is clear that Dworkin has a more complex understanding of the way in which 'rights as trumps' settle moral and political disputes.

Chapter 4   Liberalism and Liberty

1   For a discussion of the way in which ideas of freedom have come to dominate contemporary British conservative thinking, see P. Kelly, 'Ideas and Policy Agendas in Contemporary Politics', in P. Dunleavy, A. Gamble, R. Heffernan and G. Peele (eds), *Developments in British Politics*, 7, Basingstoke, Palgrave, 2003, pp. 242–60.

2   For positive and negative liberty, see I. Berlin, 'Two Concepts of Liberty', in I. Berlin, *Four Essays on Liberty*, Oxford, Oxford University Press, 1969; the republican conception of freedom is defended in Q. Skinner, *Liberty Before Liberalism*, Cambridge, Cambridge University Press, 1998, and P. Pettit, *Republicanism*, Oxford, Clarendon Press, 1997.

3   It is one of the arguments of Q. Skinner's *Liberty before Liberalism* that modern liberalism develops with a purely negative conception of liberty, and that we can trace this to the emergence of liberalism in Britain with the rise of utilitarianism from Bentham onwards. I have challenged this view in P. Kelly, 'Classical Utilitarianism and the Concept of Freedom: A Response to the Republican Critique', *Journal of Political Ideologies*, 6 (2001), 13–31.

4   Hobbes, *Leviathan*, ed. R. Tuck, Cambridge, Cambridge University Press, 1991, pp. 97–8.

5   R. Nozick, *Anarchy, State and Utopia*, Oxford, Blackwell, 1974, p. 169.

6   Bishop Butler, *Fifteen Sermons*, quoted in G. E. Moore, *Principia Ethica*, revised edn, ed. T. Baldwin, Cambridge, Cambridge University Press, 1993, p. 29.

7   J.-J. Rousseau, 'The Social Contract', in *The Social Contract and Discourses*, ed. G. D. H. Cole, London, Dent, 1955.

8   J. L. Talmon, *The Origins of Totalitarian Democracy*, New York, Praeger, 1960.

9   C. Taylor, 'What's Wrong with Negative Liberty?', in *Philosophy and the Human Sciences: Philosophical Papers*, vol. 2, Cambridge, Cambridge University Press, 1985, pp. 211–29.

10   For a comprehensive overview of the republican tradition, see J. Maynor, *Republicanism in the Modern World*, Cambridge, Polity, 2003.

11   M. Viroli, *Republicanism*, New York, Henry Holt, 2002.

12   P. Pettit, 'Negative Liberty, Liberal and Republican', *European Journal of Philosophy*, 1 (1993), 17.

13   P. Pettit, *Republicanism*, revised edn, Oxford, Clarendon Press, 1997, p. 287.

14   M. Viroli, *Republicanism*, p. 6.

15   G. C. MacCallum, 'Negative and Positive Freedom', *Philosophical Review*, 76 (1967), 312–34.

16   J. Rawls, *A Theory of Justice*, Oxford, Oxford University Press, 1999, p. 60.

17   H. L. A. Hart, 'Rawls on Liberty and its Priority', *University of Chicago Law Review*, 40 (1973), 551–5.

18   J. Rawls, *Political Liberalism*, New York, Columbia University Press, 1993, p. 291.

19   J. Gray, *Two Faces of Liberalism*, Cambridge, Polity, 2000, pp. 78–104.

20   Much of Rawls' *A Theory of Justice* as well as *Political Liberalism* is concerned with giving reasons for what might count as a member of the set of equal basic liberty. Similarly, Barry's *Culture and Equality*, Cambridge, Polity, 2000, can be read as a sustained analysis of the nature and limits of a liberal theory of freedom of association.

21   J. Rawls, *Potitical Liberalism*, New York, Columbia University Press, 1993, pp. 289–372.

Chapter 5   Liberalism and Equality

1   See Q. Skinner, *Liberty before Liberalism*, Cambridge, Cambridge University Press, 1998.

2   J. Locke, *Two Treatises of Government*, ed. P. Laslett, Cambridge, Cambridge University Press, 1970, vol. II, sect. 6, p. 270.

3   J. S. Mill, *Principles of Political Economy*, ed. J. Riley, Oxford, Oxford University Press, 1994, p. 5.

4   F. A. Hayek, *The Road to Serfdom*, London, Routledge and Kegan Paul, 1944.

5   F. A. Hayek, *The Mirage of Social Justice*, London, Routledge and Kegan Paul, 1976. Hayek's argument is restated in K. Minogue, 'Social Justice in Theory and Practice', in D. Boucher and P. Kelly (eds), *Social Justice from Hume to Walzer*, London, Routledge, 1998, pp. 253–66. The kernel of Hayek's argument is captured in Mrs Thatcher's infamous claim that 'There is no such thing as society'.

6   Rawls, *A Theory of Justice*, rev. edn, Oxford, Oxford University Press, 1999, sect. 46, p. 266.

7 For a good overview of egalitarian arguments that relativities do matter, see A. Swift, *Political Philosophy*, Cambridge, Polity, 2001, pp. 106–14.

8 The classic discussion of Rawls' failure to derive the difference principle from choice behind the veil of ignorance is B. Barry, *The Liberal Theory of Justice*, Oxford, Oxford University Press, 1973. See also P. Kelly, 'Contractarian Social Justice: An Overview of Some Contemporary Debates', in D. Boucher and P. Kelly (eds), *Social Justice from Hume to Walzer*, London Routledge, 1998, pp. 182–8.

9 Dworkin's liberal egalitarian theory of justice is set out in a number of influential articles which have recently been republished in book form as *Sovereign Virtue*, Cambridge, MA, Belknap/ Harvard University Press, 2000.

10 An exception is G. A. Cohen: see Cohen, 'On the Currency of Egalitarian Justice', *Ethics*, 99 (1989), 906–44. Cohen does want to compensate for expensive choices that are merely expensive in relation to some arbitrary societal norm or convention.

11 Dworkin, *Sovereign Virtue*, pp. 65–70.

12 Dworkin, *Sovereign Virtue*, pp. 67–8 and 139–41.

13 Dworkin, *Sovereign Virtue*, pp. 73–83 and 100–4.

14 Cohen, 'On the Currency of Egalitarian Justice', *Ethics*, 99 (1989), 906–44, and W. Kymlicka, *Liberalism, Community and Culture*, Oxford, Clarendon Press, 1989.

15 Kymlicka, *Liberalism, Community and Culture*, and *Multicultural Citizenship*, Oxford, Oxford University Press, 1995.

16 For an excellent overview of the issues involved here, see M. Matravers, 'The "Equality of What?" Debate', *Political Studies*, 50 (2002), 558–72.

17 Dworkin, *Sovereign Virtue*, pp. 287–99. Brian Barry offers a similar argument in 'Choice, Chance and Justice', in *Liberty and Justice: Essays in Political Theory*, Oxford, Oxford University Press, 1991, pp. 142–58.

18 See Matravers, 'The "Equality of What?" Debate', pp. 71–2.

19 H. L. A. Hart, *Punishment and Responsibility*, Oxford, Clarendon Press, 1968.

Chapter 6 How Political is Political Liberalism?

1 See J. Gray, *Enlightenment's Wake*, London, Routledge, 1995; G. Newey, *After Politics*, Basingstoke, Palgrave, 2001; B. Honig, *Political Theory and the Displacement of Politics*,

Ithaca, NY, Cornell University Press, 1993; and C. Mouffe, *The Return of the Political*, London, Verso, 1993.

2 M. Oakeshott, *Rationalism in Politics* (expanded edn), Indianapolis, Liberty Press, 1991; and C. Schmitt, *The Concept of the Political*, ed. G. Schwab, New Brunswick, NJ, Rutgers University Press, 1976.

3 J. Dunn, *Rethinking Modern Political Theory*, Cambridge, Cambridge University Press, 1985, and *The Cunning of Unreason*, London, Harper Collins, 2000.

4 B. Parekh, 'Theorizing Political Theory', in N. O'Sullivan (ed), *Political Theory in Transition*, London, Routledge, 2000, pp. 242–59.

5 For the best overview of Oakeshott's peculiar and complex philosophy, see D. Boucher, 'Oakeshott', in D. Boucher and P. Kelly (eds), *Political Thinkers*, Oxford, Oxford University Press, 2003, pp. 459–79.

6 B. Parekh, *Rethinking Multiculturalism*, Basingstoke, Macmillan, 2000.

7 J. Gray, *Two Faces of Liberalism*, Cambridge, Polity, 2000, 69–104.

8 B. Honig, *Political Theory and the Displacement of Politics*, pp. 126–61.

9 Newey, *After Politics*, p. 25.

10 A. MacIntyre, *After Virtue*, London, Duckworth, 1981.

11 Newey, *After Politics*, p. 24.

12 MacIntyre, *After Virtue*, pp. 74–8.

13 Newey, *After Politics*, pp. 26–31.

14 Agonistic politics sees politics as a realm of struggle between ineradicably conflictual ends. Among the most prominent theorists of agonistic politics are Mouffe, Gray and Honig. See also W. Connolly, *Identity/Difference: Democratic Negotiations of Political Paradox*, Ithaca, NY, Cornell University Press, 1991.

15 Schmitt, *The Concept of the Political*, ed, G. Schwab, New Brunswick, NJ, Rutgers University Press, 1976, p. 29.

16 Ibid., p. 71.

17 Bishop Butler, *Fifteen Sermons*, quoted in G. E. Moore, *Principia Ethica*, revised edn, ed. G. Baldwin, Cambridge, Cambridge University Press, 1993, p. 29.

18 Newey, *After Politics*, p. 31.

Chapter 7 False Neutrality and Ethnocentrism

1 The main communitarian thinkers are Michael Sandel, Alasdair MacIntyre, Charles Taylor and Michael Walzer. See

M. Sandel, *Liberalism and the Limits of Justice*, Cambridge, Cambridge University Press, 1982; A. MacIntyre, *After Virtue*, London, Duckworth, 1981, and *Whose Justice? Which Rationality?*, London, Duckworth, 1988; C. Taylor, *Sources of the Self*, Cambridge, Cambridge University Press, 1990; and M. Walzer, *Spheres of Justice*, Oxford, Blackwell, 1983. For the best overview of communitarianism in political theory, see S. Mulhall and A. Swift, *Liberals and Communitarians*, 2nd edn, Oxford, Blackwell, 1996.

2   Multiculturalist thinkers include Will Kymlicka, Chandran Kukathas, Bhikhu Parekh, James Tully and Iris Marion Young. See W. Kymlicka, *Liberalism, Community and Culture*, Oxford, Clarendon Press, 1989; C. Kukathas, *The Liberal Archipelago*, Oxford, Oxford University Press, 2003; B. Parekh, *Rethinking Multiculturalism*, Basingstoke, Macmillan, 2000; J. Tully, *Strange Multiplicity*, Cambridge, Cambridge University Press, 1995; I. Marion Young, *Justice and the Politics of Difference*, Princeton, Princeton University Press, 1990.

3   Stephen Lukes credits the late Martin Hollis as the source of this aphorism: Lukes, *Liberals and Cannibals: The Implications of Diversity*, London, Verso, 2003, p. 27. Lukes also provides an insightful account of the sources of the ethnocentric criticism in anthropology: *Liberal and Cannibals*, pp. 10–26. Though I draw different conclusions I have benefited from Lukes' discussion.

4   For a discussion of the problems of exporting liberalism to eastern Europe, see the essays in W. Kymlicka and M. Opalski (eds), *Can Liberal Pluralism be Exported?*, Oxford, Oxford University Press, 2001.

5   Tully, *Strange Multiplicity*, ch. 3; see also D. Ivison, *Postcolonial Liberalism*, Cambridge, Cambridge University Press, 2002.

6   See especially B. Parekh, *Rethinking Multiculturalism*, pp. 179–236.

7   J. Gray, *Two Faces of Liberalism*, Cambridge, Polity, 2000.

8   For an account of the ineliminability of prejudice, see H. G. Gadamer, *Truth and Method*, London, Sheed and Ward, 1965.

9   MacIntyre, *Whose Justice? Which Rationality?*, pp. 1–11.

10   Newey, *After Politics*, Basingstoke, Palgrave, 2001, pp. 138–58.

11   One of the most forceful exponents of this form of liberal critique is John Gray: see Gray, *Two Faces of Liberalism*, pp. 34–68.

12 D. Davidson, 'On the Very Idea of a Conceptual Scheme', in *Inquiries into Truth and Interpretation*, Oxford, Oxford University Press, 1984, pp. 183–98.

13 I owe this example to Professor Qiang Li of Peking University, Beijing. See Qiang Li, 'The Principle of Utility and the Principle of Righteousness: Yen Fu and Utilitarianism in Modern China', *Utilitas*, 8 (1996), 109–26.

14 S. Benhabib, *The Claims of Culture: Equality and Diversity in the Global Era*, Princeton, Princeton University Press, 2002.

15 A. Kuper, *Culture: The Anthropologists' Account*, Cambridge, MA, Harvard University Press, 1999.

16 See especially B. Parekh, *Rethinking Multiculturalism*, and J. Tully, *Strange Multiplicity*.

17 John Gray, *Two Faces of Liberalism*; J. Raz, *The Morality of Freedom*, Oxford, Clarendon Press, 1986; and Isaiah Berlin, *Two Concepts of Liberty*, Oxford, Oxford University Press, 1958.

18 MacIntyre, *Whose Justice? Which Rationality?*; C. Taylor, *Sources of the Self*, Cambridge, Cambridge University Press, 1990; and M. Walzer, *Interpretation and Social Criticism*, Cambridge, MA, Harvard University Press, 1987.

19 For a robust critique of Rawls *Political Liberalism*, see B. Barry, 'John Rawls and the Search for Stability', *Ethics*, 105 (1995), 874–915. One can argue that this is not necessarily the most charitable interpretation of Rawls, in that he does provide independent reasons for the idea of justice as fairness as a free-standing doctrine. The problem is that if the free-standing doctrine is supposed to do any serious work it must have priority, in which case the overlapping consensus seems redundant. If justice as fairness is merely one candidate for an overlapping consensus, then Rawls has indeed made his case for justice as fairness unnecessarily precarious.

Chapter 8 Liberalism, the State and Beyond

1 See I. Marion Young, *Justice and the Politics of Difference*, Princeton, Princeton University Press, 1990; J. Tully, *Strange Multiplicity*, Cambridge, Cambridge University Press, 1995; and B. Parekh, *Rethinking Multiculturalism*, Basingstoke, Macmillan, 2000.

2 The emergence of the modern juridical state and its obscurance of alternative conceptions of political associations has been a chief preoccupation of the historiography of Q. Skinner. See

Skinner, *The Foundations of Modern Political Theory*, 2 vols, Cambridge, Cambridge University Press, 1978, and *Visions of Politics*, 3 vols, Cambridge, Cambridge Unversity Press, 2002. A similar analysis of the centrality of sovereignty to contemporary theories of the state can be found in D. Held, *Democracy and the Global Order*, Cambridge, Polity, 1995.

3   The dominance of realism is by no means uncontested in international relations theory, but it still exerts a strong pull on popular thinking about international politics. For an analysis and critique of the realist paradigm in international relations theory (and much else besides), see C. J. Brown, *Sovereignty, Rights and Justice*, Cambridge, Polity, 2002.

4   M. Walzer, *Spheres of Justice*, Oxford, Blackwell, 1983, and *Interpretation and Social Criticism*, Cambridge, MA, Harvard University Press, 1987. What follows draws upon ideas developed in P. Kelly, 'Contractarian Social Justice', in D. Boucher and P. Kelly (eds), *Social Justice from Hume to Walzer*, London, Routledge, 1998, pp. 188–94.

5   Young, *Justice and the Politics of Difference*.

6   Young's influence has been considerable in modern feminist political theory: see J. Squires, *Gender in Political Theory*, Cambridge, Polity, 1999.

7   This argument is made by a number of different feminist political theorists, who use insights about gender to challenge the dominant paradigm of liberal justice: see N. Frazer, *Justus Interruptus*, New York, Routledge, 1997; and A. Phillips, *Which Equalities Matter?*, Cambridge, Polity, 1999.

8   Young's multiculturalism is more concerned with the issue of new social movements than with 'culture' as the reified identities of immigrant ethnicities. Parekh in particular differentiates his conception of culture from that of Young, in B. Parekh, 'The Logic of Intercultural Evaluation', in J. Horton and S. Mendus (eds), *Toleration, Identity and Difference*, Basingstoke, Macmillan, 1999, p. 163.

9   D. Ivison, P. Patton and W. Sanders (eds), *Political Theory and the Rights of Indigenous Peoples*, Cambridge, Cambridge University Press, 2000; and D. Ivison, *Postcolonial Liberalism*, Cambridge, Cambridge University Press, 2002.

10   See D. Runcimann, *Pluralism and the Personality of the State*, Cambridge, Cambridge University Press, 1997.

11   For an extended discussion of this problem in Parekh's multicultural theory, see P. Kelly, 'Identity, Equality and Power: Tensions in Parekh's Political Theory of Multiculturalism', in B. Haddock and P. Sutch (eds), *Multiculturalism, Identity and Rights*, London, Routledge, 2003, pp. 93–110.

12 For the most thorough discussion of this issue, see the liberal feminist Susan Moller Okin, 'Is Multiculturalism Bad for Women?', and the responses, in S. Moller Okin (ed.), *Is Multiculturalism Bad for Women?*, Princeton, Princeton University Press, 1999.

13 J. Rawls, *The Law of Peoples*, Cambridge, MA, Harvard University Press, 1999, and R. Dworkin, *Sovereign Virtue*, Cambridge, MA, Belknap/Harvard University Press, 2000.

14 Major cosmopolitan thinkers include Brian Barry, David Held, Thomas Pogge and Peter Singer: see, B. Barry, 'Statism and Nationalism: A Cosmopolitan Critique', in I. Shapiro and L. Brilmayer (eds), *Global Justice, NOMOS LXI*, New York, New York University Press, 1999, pp. 12–66; D. Held, *Democracy and the Global Order*, Cambridge, Polity, 1995, and D. Held and A. McGrew, *Globalization/Anti-Globalization*, Cambridge, Polity, 2002; T. Pogge, *World Poverty and Human Rights*, Cambridge, Polity, 2002; and P. Singer, *One World*, New Haven, Yale University Press, 2002.

15 See Barry, 'Statism and Nationalism: A Cosmpolitan Critique'; C. J. Brown, *Sovereignty, Rights and Justice*, pp. 57–76; and S. Lawson, *International Relations*, Cambridge, Polity, 2003, pp. 1–20.

16 Ethical particularists such as David Miller claim that in the one case we have obligations of justice, whereas in the other (regarding non-nationals) we have different and less urgent obligations – perhaps obligations of charity. See D. Miller, *On Nationality*, Oxford, Oxford University Press, 1995, and *Principles of Social Justice*, Cambridge, MA, Harvard University Press, 1999.

17 Consequently, I regard Rawls' *The Law of Peoples*, Cambridge, MA, Harvard University Press, 1999, as a departure from his earlier liberalism.

18 D. Held, *Democracy and the Global Order*, Cambridge, Polity, 1995, and D. Held and A. McGrew, *Globalization/Anti-Globalization*, Cambridge, Polity, 2002, pp. 88–97.

19 If there is a duty to intervene to enforce human rights this must apply equally in non-mineral rich countries as it does with respect to states that have huge oil deposits.

20 D. Held and A. McGrew, *Globalization/Anti-Globalization*; and P. Singer, *One World*, New Haven, Yale University Press, 2002.

21 See D. Held, A. McGrew, D. Goldblatt and J. Perraton, *Global Transformations*, Cambridge, Polity, 1999; and D. Held and A. McGrew (eds), *Globalization/Anti-Globalization*, Cambridge, Polity, 2002.

References

Arblaster, A. 1984: *The Rise and Decline of Western Liberalism*, Oxford, Blackwell.

Barker, R. 1990: *Political Legitimacy and the State*, Oxford, Clarendon Press.

Barker, R. 2001: *Legitimating Identities*, Cambridge, Cambridge University Press.

Barry, B. M. 1973: *The Liberal Theory of Justice*, Oxford, Oxford University Press.

Barry, B. M. 1990: 'How Not to Defend Liberal Institutions', in R. B. Douglass, G. M. Mara and H. S. Richardson (eds), *Liberalism and the Good*, New York, Routledge, pp. 44–58.

Barry, B. M. 1991: 'Choice, Chance and Justice', in *Liberty and Justice: Essays in Political Theory*, Oxford, Oxford University Press, pp. 142–58.

Barry, B. M. 1995: *Justice as Impartiality*, Oxford, Clarendon Press.

Barry, B. M. 1995: 'John Rawls and the Search for Stability', *Ethics*, 105, 874–915.

Barry, B. M. 1998: 'Something in the Disputation Not Unpleasant', in P. Kelly (ed.), *Impartiality, Neutrality and Justice*, Edinburgh, Edinburgh University Press.

Barry, B. M. 1999: 'Statism and Nationalism: A Cosmopolitan Critique', in I. Shapiro and L. Brilmayer (eds), *Global Justice: NOMOS XLI*, New York, New York University Press, pp. 12–67.

Barry, B. M. 2000: *Culture and Equality*, Cambridge, Polity.

Beiner, R. 1992: *What's the Matter with Liberalism?*, Berkeley, CA, University of California Press.

Benhabib, S. 2002: *The Claims of Culture: Equality and Diversity in the Global Era*, Princeton, Princeton University Press.

Berger, F. 1984: *Happiness, Justice and Freedom*, Berkeley, CA, University of California Press.

Berlin, I. 1958: *Two Concepts of Liberty*, Oxford, Oxford University Press.

Berlin, I. 1969: *Four Essays on Liberty*, Oxford, Oxford University Press.

Boucher, D. 2003: 'Oakeshott', in D. Boucher and P. Kelly (eds), *Political Thinkers*, Oxford, Oxford University Press.

Brown, C. J. 2002: *Sovereignty, Rights and Justice*, Cambridge, Polity.

Cohen, G. A. 1989: 'On the Currency of Egalitarian Justice', *Ethics*, 99, 906–44.

Cohen, G. A. 1997: 'Where the Action is: On the Site of Distributive Justice', *Philosophy and Public Affairs*, 26, 3–30.

Connolly, W. 1991: *Identity/Difference: Democratic Negotiations of Political Paradox*, Ithaca, NY, Cornell University Press.

Coons, J. E. and Berman, P. M. 1999: *By Nature Equal*, Princeton, Princeton University Press.

Davidson, D. 1984: 'On the Very Idea of a Conceptual Scheme', in *Inquiries into Truth and Interpretation*, Oxford, Oxford University Press.

Dunn, J. 1969: *The Political Thought of John Locke: An Historical Account of the Argument of the Two Treatises of Government*, Cambridge, Cambridge University Press.

Dunn, J. 1977: *Western Political Theory in the Face of the Future*, Cambridge, Cambridge University Press.

Dunn, J. 1984: *Locke*, Oxford, Oxford University Press.

Dunn, J. 1985: *Rethinking Modern Political Theory*, Cambridge, Cambridge University Press.

Dunn, J. 2000: *The Cunning of Unreason*, London, Harper Collins.

Dworkin, R. 1977: *Taking Rights Seriously*, London, Duckworth.

Dworkin, R. 1985: 'Liberalism', in *A Matter of Principle*, Oxford, Oxford University Press.

Dworkin, R. 1990: 'Foundations of Liberal Egalitarianism', in G. B. Peterson (ed.), *The Tanner Lectures on Human Values*, vol. xi, Salt Lake City, University of Utah Press.

Dworkin, R. 2000: *Sovereign Virtue*, Cambridge, MA, Belknap/Harvard University Press.

Flathman, R. E. 1994: *Thomas Hobbes: Skepticism, Individuality and Chastened Politics*, Thousand Oaks, CA, Sage.

Frazer, N. 1997: *Justus Interruptus*, New York, Routledge.

Fukuyama, F. 1992: *The End of History and the Last Man*, New York, Free Press.

Gadamer, H. G. 1965: *Truth and Method*, London, Sheed and Ward.

Gauthier, D. 1986: *Morals by Agreement*, Oxford, Clarendon Press.

Geuss, R. 2000: *History and Illusion*, Cambridge, Cambridge University Press.

Gray, J. 1984: *Liberalism*. Milton Keynes, Open University Press.

Gray, J. 1995: *Enlightenment's Wake*, London, Routledge.

Gray, J. 1997: *Endgames: Questions in Late Modern Political Theory*, Cambridge, Polity.

Gray, J. 2000: *Two Faces of Liberalism*, Cambridge, Polity.

Hall, J. A. 1987: *Liberalism*, London, Paladin.

Hare, R. M. 1981: *Moral Thinking: Its Method, Levels and Point*, Oxford, Clarendon Press.

Harris, I. 1994: *The Mind of John Locke*, Cambridge, Cambridge University Press.

Hart, H. L. A. 1968: *Punishment and Responsibility*, Oxford, Clarendon Press.

Hart, H. L. A. 1973: 'Rawls on Liberty and its Priority', *University of Chicago Law Review*, 40, 551–5.

Hayek, F. A. 1944: *The Road to Serfdom*, London, Routledge and Kegan Paul.

Hayek, F. A. 1976: *The Mirage of Social Justice*, London, Routledge and Kegan Paul.

Held, D. 1995: *Democracy and the Global Order*, Cambridge, Polity.

Held, D., McGrew, A., Goldblatt, D. and Perraton, J. 1999: *Global Transformations*, Cambridge, Polity.

Held, D. and McGrew, A. 2002: *Globalization/Anti-Globalization*, Cambridge, Polity.

Hobbes, T. [1651] 1991: *Leviathan*, ed. R. Tuck, Cambridge, Cambridge University Press.

Honig, B. 1993: *Political Theory and the Displacement of Politics*, Ithaca, NY, Cornell University Press.

Horton, J. and Mendus, S. 1999: *Toleration, Identity and Difference*, Basingstoke, Macmillan.

Ivison, D. 2002: *Postcolonial Liberalism*, Cambridge, Cambridge University Press.

Ivison, D., Patton, P. and Sanders, W. (eds) 2000: *Political Theory and the Rights of Indigenous Peoples*, Cambridge, Cambridge University Press.

Kant, Immanuel [1785] 1996: *The Groundwork of The Metaphysics of Morals*, trans. M. Gregor, in *The Cambridge Edition of the Works of Immanuel Kant: Practical Philosophy*, Cambridge, Cambridge University Press, pp. 37–108.

Kelly, P. 1990: *Utilitarianism and Distributive Justice; Jeremy Bentham and the Civil Law*, Oxford, Clarendon Press.

Kelly, P. 1997: 'Contractarian Ethics', in R. Chadwick (ed.), *Encyclopedia of Applied Ethics*, vol. 1, San Diego, Academic Press, pp. 631–43.

Kelly, P. 1998: 'Contractarian Social Justice: An Overview of Some Contemporary Debates', in D. Boucher and P. Kelly (eds), *Social Justice from Hume to Walzer*, London, Routledge.

Kelly, P. (ed.) 1998: *Impartiality, Neutrality and Justice*, Edinburgh, Edinburgh University Press.

Kelly, P. 2000: 'Political Theory in Retreat? Contemporary Political Philosophy and the Historical Order', in N. O'Sullivan (ed.), *Political Theory in Transition*, London, Routledge.

Kelly, P. 2001: 'Classical Utilitarianism and the Concept of Freedom: A Response to the Republican Critique', *Journal of Political Ideologies*, 6, 13–31.

Kelly, P. 2003: 'Ideas and Policy Agendas in Contemporary Politics', in P. Dunleavy, A. Gamble, R. Heffernan and G. Peele (eds), *Developments in British Politics*, 7, Basingstoke, Palgrave, pp. 242–60.

Kelly, P. 2003: 'Identity, Equality and Power: Tensions in Parekh's Political Theory of Multiculturalism', in B. Haddock and P. Sutch (eds), *Multiculturalism, Identity and Rights*, London, Routledge, pp. 94–110.

Kelly, P. and Boucher, D. 1994: 'The Social Contract and its Critics', in D. Boucher and P. Kelly (eds), *The Social Contract from Hobbes to Rawls*, London, Routledge.

Korsgaard, C. M. 1996: *The Sources of Normativity*, Cambridge, Cambridge University Press.

Kukathas, C. 2003: *The Liberal Archipelago*, Oxford, Oxford, University Press.

Kuper, A. 1999: *Culture: The Anthropologist's Account*, Cambridge, MA, Harvard University Press.

Kymlicka, W. 1989: *Liberalism, Community and Culture*, Oxford, Clarendon Press.

Kymlicka, W. 1995: *Multicultural Citizenship*, Oxford, Oxford University Press.

Kymlicka, W. and Opalski, M. (eds) 2001: *Can Liberal Pluralism be Exported?*, Oxford, Oxford University Press.

Lawson, S. 2003: *International Relations*, Cambridge, Polity.

Locke, J. [1689] 1970: *Two Treatises of Government*, ed. P. Laslett, Cambridge, Cambridge University Press.

Locke, J. [1689] 1975: *An Essay Concerning Human Understanding*, ed. P. H. Nidditch, Oxford, Clarendon Press.

Lukes, S. 2003: *Liberals and Cannibals: The Implications of Diversity*, London, Verso.

MacCallum, G. C. 1967: 'Negative and Positive Freedom', *Philosophical Review*, 76, 312–34.

MacIntyre, A. 1981: *After Virtue*, London, Duckworth.

MacIntyre, A. 1988: *Whose Justice? Which Rationality?*, London, Duckworth.

Matravers, M. 2002: 'The "Equality of What?" Debate', *Political Studies*, 50, 558–72.

Maynor, J. 2003: *Republicanism in the Modern World*, Cambridge, Polity.

Mendus, S. L. 1998: 'Some Mistakes about Impartiality', in P. Kelly (ed.), *Impartiality, Neutrality and Justice*, Edinburgh, Edinburgh University Press.

Mill, J. S. 1991: 'On Liberty', in J. Gray (ed.), *John Stuart Mill On Liberty and other Essays*, Oxford, Oxford University Press.

Mill, J. S. 1994: *Principles of Political Economy*, ed. J. Riley, Oxford, Oxford University Press.

Miller, D. 1995: *On Nationality*, Oxford, Oxford University Press.

Miller, D. 1999: *Principles of Social Justice*, Cambridge, MA, Harvard University Press.

Minogue, K. 1998: 'Social Justice in Theory and Practice', in D. Boucher and P. Kelly (eds), *Social Justice from Hume to Walzer*, London, Routledge, pp. 253–66.

Moore, G. E. [1903] 1993: *Principia Ethica*, revised edn, ed. T. Baldwin, Cambridge, Cambridge University Press.

Mouffe, C. 1993: *The Return of the Political*, London, Verso.

Mulhall, S. and Swift, A. 1996: *Liberals and Communitarians*, Oxford, Blackwell.

Neal, P. 1997: *Liberalism's Discontents*, Basingstoke, Macmillan.

Newey, G. 2001: *After Politics*, Basingstoke, Palgrave.

Nozick, R. 1974: *Anarchy, State and Utopia*, Oxford, Blackwell.

Oakeshott, M. 1991: *Rationalism in Politics*, ed. T. Fuller, Indianapolis, Liberty Press.

Okin, S. Moller 1999: *Is Multiculturalism Bad for Women?*, Princeton, Princeton University Press.

O'Neill, O. 1989: *Constructions of Reason*, Cambridge, Cambridge University Press.

Parekh, B. 2000: 'Theorizing Political Theory', in N. O'Sullivan (ed.), *Political Theory in Transition*, London, Routledge, pp. 242–59.

Parekh, B. 2000: *Rethinking Multiculturalism*, Basingstoke, Macmillan.

Pettit, P. 1993: 'Negative Liberty, Liberal and Republican', *European Journal of Philosophy*, 1, 17.

Pettit, P. 1997: *Republicanism*, Oxford, Clarendon Press.

Phillips, A. 1999: *Which Equalities Matter?* Cambridge, Polity.

Pogge, T. 2002: *World Poverty and Human Rights*, Cambridge, Polity.

Qiang, L. 1996: 'The Principle of Utility and the Principle of Righteousness: Yen Fu and Utilitarianism in Modern China', *Utilitas*, 8, 109–26.

Rawls, J. 1999: *A Theory of Justice*, Oxford, Oxford University Press.

Rawls, J. 1993: *Political Liberalism*, New York, Columbia University Press.

Rawls, J. 1999: *The Law of Peoples*, Cambridge, MA, Harvard University Press.

Raz, J. 1986: *The Morality of Freedom*, Oxford, Clarendon Press.

Raz, J. 2003: *The Practice of Value*, Oxford, Clarendon Press.

Rousseau, J.-J. [1754,1755,1762] 1955: *The Social Contract and Discourses*, ed. G. D. H. Cole, London, Dent.

Runcimann, D. 1997: *Pluralism and the Personality of the State*, Cambridge, Cambridge University Press.

Sandel, M. 1982: *Liberalism and the Limits of Justice*, Cambridge, Cambridge University Press.

Sandel, M. 1995: *Democracy's Discontent*, Cambridge, MA, Harvard University Press.

Scanlon, T. M. 1982: 'Contractualism and Utilitarianism', in A. Sen and B. Williams (eds), *Utilitarianism and Beyond*, Cambridge, Cambridge University Press.

Scanlon, T. M. 1999: *What We Owe to Each Other*, Cambridge, MA, Belknap/Harvard University Press.

Schmitt, C. 1976: *The Concept of the Political*, ed. G. Schwab, New Brunswick, NJ, Rutgers University Press.

Singer, P. 2002: *One World*, New Haven, Yale University Press.

Skinner, Q. 1978: *The Foundations of Modern Political Theory*, 2 vols, Cambridge, Cambridge University Press.

Skinner, Q. 1998: *Liberty Before Liberalism*, Cambridge, Cambridge University Press.

Skinner, Q. 2002: *Visions of Politics*, vol. 1: *Regarding Method*, Cambridge, Cambridge University Press.

Smith, A. [1759] 1976: *The Theory of Moral Sentiments*, ed. D. D. Raphael and A. L. Macfie, Oxford, Clarendon Press.

Squires, J. 1999: *Gender in Political Theory*, Cambridge, Polity.

Steiner, H. 1995: *An Essay on Rights*, Oxford, Blackwell.

Swift, A. 2001: *Political Philosophy*, Cambridge, Polity.

Talmon, J. L. 1960: *The Origins of Totalitarian Democracy*, New York, Praeger.

Taylor, C. 1985: 'What's Wrong with Negative Liberty?', in *Philosophy and the Human Sciences: Philosophical Papers*, vol. 2, Cambridge, Cambridge University Press, pp. 211–29.

Taylor, C. 1990: *Sources of the Self*, Cambridge, Cambridge University Press.

Temkin, L. 1993: *Inequality*, Oxford, Oxford University Press.

Tully, J. 1995: *Strange Multiplicity*, Cambridge, Cambridge University Press.

Viroli, M. 2002: *Republicanism*, New York, Henry Holt.

Waldron, J. 1988: *Liberal Rights*, Cambridge, Cambridge University Press.

Waldron, J. 2002: *God, Locke and Equality*, Cambridge, Cambridge University Press.

Waldron, J. 2003: 'John Locke', in D. Boucher and P. Kelly (eds), *Political Thinkers*, Oxford, Oxford University Press.

Walzer, M. 1983: *Spheres of Justice*, Oxford, Blackwell.

Walzer, M. 1987: *Interpretation and Social Criticism*, Cambridge, MA, Harvard University Press.

Williams, B. 1973: 'A Critique of Utilitarianism', in B. Williams and J. J. C. Smart (eds), *Utilitarianism: For and Against*, Cambridge, Cambridge University Press.

Williams, B. 1985: *Ethics and the Limits of Philosophy*, London, Fontana.

Young, I. M. 1990: *Justice and the Politics of Difference*, Princeton, Princeton University Press.

Index